LEADING THROUGH THE HEAT

Essential Leadership Lessons from the Firehouse to the Corporate World

Mark Andrew

Published by Freiling Agency, LLC.

P.O. Box 1264
Warrenton, VA 20188

www.FreilingAgency.com

PB ISBN: 978-1-969826-10-8
E-book ISBN: 978-1-969826-11-5

Contents

Preface...v

1 Lucky..1

2 What Makes a Good Leader? 9

3 Learning to Lead...23

4 Making the Transition................................35

5 Poor Worker or Poor Leader? 47

6 Poor Worker Is Just a Poor Worker.........59

7 A Confident Leader 77

8 Modern Management at the Firehouse? ...91

9 Take from the Good 103

10 Presence vs. Micromanaging 115

11 The Crew's Trust 127

12 Cultivate Integrity.................................143

13 Breach of Trust......................................155

14 Walk with Purpose................................163

Conclusion..177

Acknowledgments 179

Preface

I finally did it. I sat down and found a balance between motivation and discipline. After years of writing essays that never gained traction or even got published, I struggled with whether I could call myself a writer. However, that changed when I was invited to be a guest on some excellent fire service podcasts. While taking notes for talking points, I realized they could be transformed into articles for various magazines and websites. Inspired, I decided to knuckle down and write a book. It was both exciting and cathartic, and surprisingly easier than I had expected. I am passionate about this material, and I enjoyed compiling my thoughts and reflecting on past experiences to turn them into lessons for others aspiring to be leaders.

I genuinely believe I have the greatest job in the world. The fire service has given me so much more than I could ever give back to it. Please don't interpret the anecdotes about leadership issues in the first chapter as bitterness or resentment; they are quite the opposite. I have learned valuable lessons and hope those in leadership positions can learn from them as well. No one is perfect—certainly not me—but I hope that everyone can benefit from the lessons I've shared.

These connections have transformed not only the way I view teamwork but also how I approach personal growth. The shared laughter, the brainstorming sessions, and even the disagreements have all played a part in forging bonds that will last far beyond this endeavor. As I reflect on the stories etched into my experiences, I realize how they intertwine with the experiences of others.

The names in the first chapter have been changed. As I mentioned before, I don't share these experiences with any animosity—instead, I express my genuine appreciation for the opportunities to learn and improve throughout my career. However, the names of the officers from whom I learned significant lessons are real. I wanted to ensure that these dedicated officers receive credit for their leadership effectiveness and for the examples they set for me.

Some of the interactions mentioned in this book were fleeting, others profound. Yet they all carried a weight of significance. It's fascinating how our individual narratives can come together, creating lessons of shared human experience that we can take lessons from. The stories of successes and struggles resonate deeply and remind me that we are all growing and learning every day in whatever career we are in. This journey of completing a career in the fire service is a testament to the power of not only perseverance but also passion for the work. It reinforces my unwavering belief that sharing our stories can lead to inspiration and growth—not just for ourselves but for those who follow in our footsteps.

As I reflect on this journey, I feel a deep sense of accomplishment not just in the final product but in the lessons learned, the relationships built, and the stories etched into my experiences. It's a testament to the power of perseverance, passion, and the unwavering belief that sharing our stories can lead to inspiration and growth—for ourselves and for those who follow in our footsteps.

Each challenge faced has shaped my perspective, instilling resilience and a sense of purpose that I carry with me and hope to use to make the fire service better for those who come after me. The 911 calls, the relationships, and the conversations at the kitchen table all contributed to a richer narrative—one that is as much about the process as it is about the outcome.

By openly discussing my journey, I hope to encourage others to embrace their own paths, face their own challenges, and ultimately find their voices. In the end, this experience has been about much more than achieving a goal; it's been about the transformation that occurs within us and the impact we can have when we share our truths with others. I carry forward this sense of responsibility to inspire, uplift, and connect, knowing that each story has the potential to spark change and cultivate understanding in a world that thrives on connection. Above all, to make the fire service and any workplace better for those who come after us.

Without these experiences, I wouldn't be the officer I am today, and for that, I will always be thankful. I would also like to extend my gratitude to one individual outside the fire service—my editor, Michael Tizzano. I quickly realized that I needed the skilled eye of a literary professional to help with structure and grammar, as I am good at my job but lack the skills of a copy editor. I also appreciate Michael's patience in not searching for my address, showing up at my house, and strangling me for my inability to properly use a colon or semicolon.

His unwavering support and keen eye for detail have genuinely made a difference in transforming my thoughts into a polished manuscript. More than that, he believed in the project from the beginning. Thank you, Michael.

> Lead me, follow me, or get out of my way.
>
> —*General George Patton*

1

Lucky

I've been lucky. I've worked with some horrible bosses. I didn't realize until I joined the fire service that I shouldn't dwell on or be frustrated by the myriad of poor management debacles, because these experiences are some of the best to learn from.

When I was a junior firefighter, we were dispatched to a house fire. I am assigned to the ambulance, which has gear and tools as part of the standard box alarm we send to every building fire. It's a great job, but the best assignment and the one everyone wants is the first due fire engine.

The first engine is the crew to bring the hose line into the building and attack the fire. We have ladder trucks that can ventilate the structure or search for victims. Rescue companies (ambulances) are often assigned other tasks, such as helping outside or going in with a second hoseline, which can lead to some exciting work.

However, the critical thing to understand is everyone wants to be inside on that hose line. It's by far the most fun, exciting, and rewarding thing we do: stopping the fire from spreading and saving lives and property, all while being in the heat and hitting it. We don't get to do it every day. Being inside is the best job I've ever had, and it is nearly unheard of to be assigned it and pass it off.

This house fire was one of those nearly unheard-of calls. The officer on the first due engine, mostly due to injury, didn't want to go in and took time to do a size-up and survey. When the second arriving rig showed up, he was willing to hand the hose line off to them. What turned eye-opening for me was that as his partner was putting his mask and hood on to get ready, the officer opened the side door to find an obvious basement fire. As the black smoke poured out the door, the firefighter off the second arriving rig, Mark, was approaching the side door. The officer was on a knee, holding the hose, coat half open, no mask on, then pointed downstairs and said, "It's down there." Mark, who is rather tall and imposing, stood over the officer, stared down at him, and shouted:

"You fucking think so, Larry?"

Then, he grabbed the nozzle, went downstairs, and put out the fire.

Three things happened here:

1. He stood over him

2. Yelled at a senior officer

3. Refused to call him by his rank and used his first name on a fire scene.

Not a week later, after I had time to reflect, not later in the day as things calmed down, but right there in the moment, I remember saying to myself,

"I am never going to be that guy."

I knew right away I never wanted to be the guy who would send in a crew to a place he did not want to go himself. I would never be the guy who would not want to go into a fire. And I would never be the officer who would let my crew see me being timid.

As I said, it was lucky for me because examples of poor leadership like this happened a few more times before I was promoted to company officer.

The following formative incident was when I was a senior firefighter, having had my first promotion, and was on a crew with a newer lieutenant. While he was a nice enough man, he wasn't a good fire officer and was promoted in an era of a competitive exam that leaned more towards book smarts than work experience. This officer struggled with a lot of things, and as I found out, the chain of command was one of them.

My Captain had been tasked with setting up some schedules for our unit, and he gave them to the lieutenant, who then delegated it to me. We had just gone from paper and transcribing the shift's days off on a calendar to a computer form. To my frustration, the computer sheet was edited by someone else, causing the schedule to be off. As a result, when others tried to request time off, it left us with too many absences, and people had to be denied their time. After some digging, I discovered that the local document I thought I was using was a shared document on a public drive. This meant that when others accessed it, they could make edits, as we were unaware of the "read-only" function. (This is years before Google

Docs and other password-protected modern files.) I was at least happy I found the problem and devised a solution. Unfortunately, the battalion chief did not share my glass-half-full viewpoint.

The chief officer calls down to our station to chew out someone, and my new lieutenant answers the call and says Just a minute, here he is… and hands me the phone. I could hear the chief yelling at me before I even got the phone to my ear, and I sat there in shock at why the officer was not taking this call. I then spent the next three minutes stammering.

"Yes, sir….sir…..sir….yes, sir….very sorry, sir…… sir..sir..sir… won't happen again, sir."

This was interrupted by me covering the phone with my hand and yelling in a loud whisper.

"What the hell are you doing, Tommy?!"

"Yes sir…sir…sir…"

"You're supposed to be taking this call!"

Tommy, the lieutenant, says, "But it was your screwup?"

I replied, "It doesn't matter, the chain of command works down just as it works up!"

"Yes, sir… Sir… Won't happen again, sir…"

Now, of course, the chief officer was equally to blame; he could have insisted that this lieutenant stay on the phone and chewed him out, and not the junior person involved.

But either way, I knew right there in the moment if I was ever to be a boss, when my chief was mad and wanted his pound of flesh, I would stand in front of my crew and take it.

Taking responsibility as a leader means protecting your team and fostering trust and respect. It shows your willingness to shoulder challenges and shield your crew from unnecessary blame, creating a supportive and confident work environment. This approach not only strengthens team morale but also encourages accountability and growth among team members.

The bigger the badge, the bigger the shield.

Not surprisingly, it happened again with this same lieutenant. That lieutenant, Mark, who is now an engineer driving the fire truck, and I are on a car fire on the freeway. It ends up being a semi-truck fire, and the engineer is correctly worried about how much water we have, especially if the diesel tank were to rupture. He asks the lieutenant, "Hey LT, we might need some more water. Do you want to:

- call a second engine,

- or we can try to knock it down and go fill at a hydrant,

- or call the rescue company to come help us run some hose up the hill to the main road and find a hydrant?"

This was very early in the cell phone days, and the Lieutenant was the only guy I knew who had one. He said, "Give me a minute, I'll call the battalion chief." Mark takes his hand and moves the phone away from his ear, points his finger at the lieutenant's chest, and shouts

"I don't want you to make a fucking phone call! I want you to handle it!"

The lieutenant stands there, stammers, then walks away, saying he has to call the boss and see what he wants him to do.

I stand there dumbfounded, unable to believe that a company officer either couldn't make a decision or didn't want to make one. I can't believe this officer didn't care about how he was perceived, and honestly, I don't think he was even aware of how he appeared. The engineer provided three solid options for him to choose from. But for some reason, he was more afraid of what his boss would say if he made a decision that didn't work than of what his crew would think of him. Picking a course of action and adjusting as the situation changed wasn't an option. He wanted the safety of shifting the responsibility to someone else.

Every management book I have read, every fire officer class I have taken, and every leadership seminar I have attended didn't teach me as much about leadership as this one fire.

These three incidents shaped my vision of the type of company officer I wanted to be more than any class I have taken or textbook I have read.

"

He who has never learned to obey cannot
be a good commander.

—*Aristotle*

"

2

What Makes a Good Leader?

Textbooks will discuss empathy, communication, integrity, and accountability—all great thoughts and important pieces. In the fire service, though, we have a unique dynamic that emphasizes one fundamental trait: **being good at the job**.

How do you get good at the job?

The department you work for will provide plenty of opportunities to train, practice, and go on 911 calls and learn from real-life incidents. The burden, however, of getting good at the job relies solely on you.

Author Malcolm Gladwell famously wrote of the "10,000 hours" needed to master a skill. But how do you get there? Another author, Mel Robbins, says, "Nobody's coming through that door."

Nobody is coming to tell you to put down the TV remote. Nobody is coming to ask you to stop scrolling on your phone. Nobody is coming to tell you to read that promotional book or that article in a fire magazine. Nobody is coming to ask you to go to the workout room. Nobody is coming to tell you not to eat that dessert tonight. You can be as good at this job as you want; it just takes dedication.

The first route to becoming good at your job starts with the job itself, doing it every day, and always learning from every experience. In the fire and EMS services, this means taking every call seriously. (This is way harder than the general public would think, with the extraordinary amount of ridiculous non-emergency calls we go on.) Even before the call comes in, a firefighter who wants to get better can practice with their gear. They can go through the engine or ladder and continuously practice with equipment and memorize its locations. Additionally, they can run through scenarios with specialty equipment.

Even doing daily mandatory rig checks provides opportunities to learn. You can start the rig and assume everything is good and pencil-whip the checkoffs, or you can truly do a deep dive into the rig every day, put the rig through its paces, and personally start all the power tools. Know where the fluids are (and if they are leaking and need attention). Put the rig in the pump and repeat the process until the movements become muscle memory. Be the engineer who can operate their rig if the lights go out, not the one who says "It's not my fault" when the crew does not have any water. A classic joke in the fire service is at shift change when someone who is relieving you asks how the rig is, "Should be good" is the answer that would be given by someone who never actually checked it the day before. So, you can be good at the job, or you can be that guy.

Before I was hired full-time, I was in another department part-time. One scene had our ladder truck, which would self-retract if certain parts of the ladder were rotated too far when fully extended. Of course, Murphy's law kicked in, and a firefighter was on the ladder to direct the nozzle when the top section retracted and caught his leg. Luckily, he wasn't hurt, but it was a close call. During the investigation afterwards, the driver who is assigned to the rig every day said, "How am I supposed to know it does that?"

Well, I can think of a lot of reasons, but first off, **Because You Work Here.**

Once again, you can be good at the job, or you can be that guy.

How do you get good at the job of leadership, though?

In the same way, by going on calls, learning, studying, paying attention to buildings in your city, hazards in your town, and what you would do if there were ever an emergency. Early on in my career, my department responded to a fire at a hazardous material facility. When a firefighter from the first due engine got stuck in a vat of sludge and had to be pulled out and his gear thrown away, the officer in charge later said, "Well, how am I supposed to know that vat was there?"

Like I said, **Because You Work Here.**

Nevertheless, let's break that statement down a little more. "How was I supposed to know that vat was there?"

- Well, this was an industrial site that had five or six medium to large-scale incidents in the last five years.

- The company officer in charge had been assigned to the station in that district for a couple of years.

- Each year, we survey and re-survey every hazardous material site in the city, compiling a site plan that we encourage crews to train on.

- Those site plans are in a three-ring binder in every fire truck.

- The site plan for that site included a map of the site and the building, known as the Vat Building, which warned crews of the vat located near the entrance without any guardrails present.

Being good at the job can start with simply knowing your area and putting in a small amount of work studying the buildings you respond to and the equipment you respond with. Putting the work into being good at your job, more than anything else, is what earns the respect of your co-workers. Performing well on the scene, knowing what to do, and being a partner someone can count on are the first and most essential steps in earning respect.

In the fire service (outside of some administrative positions), everyone does every job as they promote up. We are also a true brotherhood- and sisterhood with all members usually being in the same association or bargaining union. Unlike the military, we don't have a code of conduct or hard rules. For instance, we don't salute officers when they enter a room, always address them by rank, or separate officers and enlisted personnel in the dining room or dorms. Military training is so thorough that the enlisted soldiers have a baked-in trust of the officers assigned to them, even if they just met them. In the fire service, there are no dictates to respect an officer. The crews have to want to do it.

With this in mind, the groundwork for being a company officer is laid years before your promotion. In most fire departments, those eligible to test for Lieutenant usually test for a few years before making it to the top of the list. This allows firefighters the time to gain the experience needed to handle scenes as an officer, making the decisions rather than following orders. It also allows firefighters to develop and demonstrate their abilities and skills to the crews they work with. It shows the troops your ability to be a good crew member, a hard worker, a good firefighter, and a good paramedic. This lays the groundwork for the trust that crews will have with an officer when the time comes.

At the fire station, we call this "transitioning to the front seat." The engineer drives the truck, and the junior firefighter rides in the back, ready to carry out the tasks assigned by the officer who sits in the front right. The view is different from up there—figuratively as much as literally.

Of course, you see more of the scene while driving there. Of course, you see the house, the traffic accident, or the medical scene. But a good officer sees much more. Possible hazards, unruly patients, traffic not stopping, fire spreading in a building, and hazards in a building that you can't see from the outside. All of these serve one purpose: to make sure your crew goes home at the end of the shift.

Unlike the military, when in battle, there are no acceptable casualties in the fire service. We perform constant and recurring "risk vs. benefit" analyses for every strategy. We "risk a lot to save a lot" and "risk a little to save a little." However, even when risking a lot, those tactics are done in such a tight and supervised manner that casualties on the fireground are still very rare. Leaders are supposed to know the fire behavior and the limits of the gear and balance that against the progress they are making. The junior firefighter with us on an interior attack is counting on our decisions to get them out to safety when the time comes.

To return to the anecdote in the first chapter, none of these analyses and decisions can be made if the officer is outside holding the door as the junior crews are inside fighting the fire. A common motivational cartoon seen on many office desks features a sled being pulled by four workers, with someone in the sled cracking a whip at the men as he is being pulled. This is labeled "Boss." The other side shows a sled being pulled by five workers, with the fifth one pointing forward as he or she pulls along with the crew. This is labeled "Leader."

It's simple, but it's true.

Speaking with a fellow company officer, Chris is his name, one day we were comparing the dynamics of each of our crews and sharing officer experiences. I was promoted a few years before him, and he was still new as a Lieutenant. I noticed when he was promoted to LT, the only opening was on his current crew, so he was a driver one day and a boss the next, in the same company. When I was promoted to officer, I immediately transferred to a new crew and had a fresh start. I asked him if being promoted to the same crew was challenging.

He said, "Nah, they know who you are by now." He was right.

Were you a firefighter who showed up early, ready to work? Were you a firefighter who was in shape and could perform on the fireground? Were you a firefighter who practiced, trained, and improved over ten to fifteen years while working for a promotion? Were you a good paramedic who knew your skills and treated your patients with respect, even when on your twentieth call and no sleep? How about around the station? Were you the guy with a positive attitude, or the one who was always bitter or angry when given an assignment you didn't like? Or were you the guy who sat in the recliner all day while the rest of your crew trained, did daily chores, and kept the rigs and equipment in order?

Because if you were not pulling your weight for fifteen years and finally promoted to Lieutenant, good luck trying to convince anyone on your crew to care about their work. Nothing goes over more like a lead balloon than an officer who turns the switch from "complainer guy" in the recliner to "Gunny Highway" overnight.

Conversely, a good leader cannot charge in on day one, bragging about all of their hard work and their demands of perfection. More military veterans that I can remember have shared with me their views of what makes a good 2nd Lieutenant. Universally, they say the best thing a new Lieutenant can do on day one is ask their sergeant, "What can I do to help you do your job?" The "new sheriff in town" mentality never wins over a crew.

Some of the most influential moments of my younger career were when, in a brutal scene, a senior firefighter or even a company officer who had "been there and done that" knew what to do, took charge, and handled the emergency. Whether it's a challenging medical scene, figuring out how to cut a mangled car open with the Jaws, or figuring out the building construction intricacies during a house fire. Seeing people who are good at the job perform at a high level is one of the best tools to motivate the young members to do the work necessary to become good themselves. Whenever I saw a solid officer make a great decision, I couldn't wait to train, to study, to read, whatever it took to make myself better.

What is different about the fire service is that seniority means a lot. Tasks are assigned based on our seniority as much as by rank. Less desirable tasks are assigned to junior members, while senior members are offered easier or more enjoyable assignments. Our first assignments as rookies in my department are to work on the ambulance, with occasional rotations on the fire engine. When assigned to the ambulance, they are partnered with someone who has more time on the job than they do. It is that time in the ambulance that begins the training of becoming a leader for a senior person. You start as the senior person on a rig with a brand-new firefighter who will look to you to be a mentor. The effectiveness of a mentorship can vary, but the key factor is that the mentor genuinely cares about the new member's growth. They want the new member to learn and become a great employee, ideally progressing to become a good officer.

Conversely, those who do not care about the new partner, don't give him or her tips on patient care, writing a report, or doing work around the station, show them how to use a power tool, share tips of the trade, and very rarely make an officer that people want to work with. It is sad when someone uses their seniority to give all the work to the rookie, not so they can learn, but so they don't have to do anything. Piling on the new guy as you sit in the recliner sends a message to the rest of the crew that you are in this for yourself. However, being engaged in training, reaching out to the rookie to see how they are doing, and taking time from your day to be that coach or mentor to someone junior to you also sends a message to the crew. These are the building blocks of leadership, and after 15 years, they "will know who you are."

These traits, this behavior, truly caring about the development of the next generation, make the crew not only stronger but safer on the fireground, and are the first step in developing the skills to lead. Nothing is worse than an officer who took the job because it's easy, they can delegate their work to others, or, most egregiously, they took it for the money.

That role of the senior firefighter carries on through a career. If you're the junior guy and we hire a new one after two years, you won't be junior anymore. It is not a promotion, but it is a step up. The newest member sees you as a senior member, and how you react is what sets you up for learning the skills of leadership. A common phrase when I was coming up the ranks, or even at prior jobs, was, "The senior guys did it to me when I was new, so it's now this guy's turn to take it."

This is death for a prospective company officer. A true leader wants to leave it better for those coming up than they had it, constantly improving not only themselves but the culture of the department they work for.

I have hobbies outside of firefighting, one of which is playing baseball in a men's recreational league. This got me thinking: as a baseball player, I will never be more than a rec league player. This is simply a hobby for me. No matter how skilled I become or how hard I train, I know that scouts are unlikely to come knocking on my door. And you know what? That's perfectly fine. I understand my strengths and weaknesses; I excel in firefighting, while hitting fastballs is not where my talents lie.

This train of thought led me to a thought experiment: if my profession, or any job for that matter, were akin to baseball, where would I rank? Would I be in the major leagues, hanging with the elite, or would I be stuck in the minor leagues, or even just another rec league player? Ideally, I would like to believe that after years of dedication and hard work, I would be in the majors—though ultimately, that assessment lies in the hands of others. For me, the aim is clear: I strive to excel in my role, continuously improving and aiming for the highest standards.

I consider myself fortunate because my jurisdiction offers abundant opportunities for professional growth. We operate a bustling department; on an average weekday, my station handles anywhere from 20 to 25 calls a day. As I sit here writing this, I've already responded to two rollover car accidents today alone—this month, we've had about seven of those. Just this week, we've also tackled a couple of fires, alongside a multitude of varied medical runs that test our skills and adaptability.

In our organization, hiring practices are somewhat unique. We rarely recruit fresh graduates right out of school. Instead, we encourage aspiring firefighters to gain relevant experience before joining our ranks. This often involves working in private EMS for medical transports, volunteering with smaller town fire departments, or even seeking positions in an emergency room. We call this time in the field the "minor leagues." These experiences are invaluable, as they give recent graduates an opportunity to work directly with patients in a non-emergency setting or assist smaller rural departments that manage a lower call volume.

By spending a couple of years in these roles, candidates refine their skills in real-world situations, allowing them to build both confidence and competence. This hands-on experience is crucial and often results in these young professionals moving up the hiring eligibility list in our department. Many continue to polish their skills over time, navigating the challenges presented in a fast-paced urban 911 environment, which can be vastly different from the experiences they encountered in their initial roles.

We're truly fortunate to have such dedicated young firefighters working alongside us. Their commitment to self-improvement not only enhances their own capabilities but also raises the standard for our team as a whole. They are driven and eager to absorb knowledge, each of them aiming to reach the pinnacle of their careers—a "major leaguer" status. This embodies our department's ethos of continuous growth and excellence.

The journey of transformation from minor leagues to major leagues differentiates the good from the exceptional. For those of us in leadership roles, it is a source of pride to be part of these individuals' professional development. Watching them grow, overcoming challenges, and eventually contributing significantly to the team's success is immensely gratifying. It's a testament to the dedication of both the leadership and the young recruits, proving that through hard work, resilience, and a desire for growth, we can all climb our own career ladders—whether that means moving from the minors to the majors in our respective fields or simply striving for excellence in whatever we do.

> When provided the opportunity
> to lead, take charge.
>
> —*General Norman Schwarzkopf*

3

Learning to Lead

General Schwarzkopf's words are great advice, but this is hard to do in practice. It is excellent advice, but hard to do. In the fire service, like most workplaces, a senior worker who wants opportunities to expand their role can be provided the chance to do so. A project manager is on vacation, a job foreman is off sick, a lead attorney is called into another case, or a Fire Lieutenant has the day off. All workplaces have times when people will step up. How you do it is certainly a learning curve, but these are the best opportunities to learn. There is a fine line between the assistant regional manager and the assistant *to* the regional manager.

When you're senior enough to be trusted with filling in for the boss, being humble will take you a long way. No one wants a "straw boss" who barks commands or tries to make policy when work needs to be done and assignments need to be carried out. Leading people to do their jobs should not be hard. For this to work, the boss needs to set the groundwork ahead of time for a crew to be self-sufficient. The senior worker filling in should not have to reinvent the wheel but simply carry on with the expectations that have already been instilled. Nothing as a boss is more satisfying than a team that can function smoothly and at a high level in your absence.

Even with a strong officer, it is still very important for senior workers to take on these roles and 'step up' for their crew and the overall mission. I have been on some crews where the senior firefighter who is not an officer (similar to a military sergeant) was the strongest leader, and the crew's identity reflected his influence. This isn't even a criticism of the officer; it simply shows the trust the captain had in this senior firefighter to delegate much of the training and daily operations so things ran smoothly and the captain did not need to intervene. This does not mean the captain can hide away in an office, but it does mean a senior worker can earn the right to take charge.

In the fire service, being senior and stepping up to fill in various roles is the best way to learn. Whether it be driving the fire truck or riding in the "in charge" seat, learning by doing works best. No textbook is going to teach every scenario or every situation, but being out there, taking 911 calls, making decisions, managing people, and learning what works and does not, yes, even making mistakes, leads to developing not only experience but people skills.

How does an officer decide the balance that exists between delegating and micromanaging?

You want to empower people for sure, but you also want to make sure you, as the leader, have set the goals and expectations you want the crew to achieve. Whether military or paramilitary, a typical structure is that the command sets out the strategy, and the crew leaders set out the tactics to achieve it.

In the fire service, this also works with our chief officers. If on the fireground, the chief wants us to ventilate a roof, I will then tell my crew what tools and ladders to grab and where to meet me to ascend to the roof. The chief will not tell me what tactics to use; the chief just wants me to accomplish the goal. The same goes for other tasks. If the chief gives me multiple things needed to get done, I can say to my partner, "Grab a line, we are going in," and tell the rescue company, "Force the door." But what I won't do is tell the rescue how to force it. I assume they remember their training, and they will size up the door and choose the right tools and tactics for breaking it down. That groundwork of trust, though, is built long before the fire.

This is where truly finding the balance of delegation is essential. The senior crew members need a leader willing to delegate around the station. This develops their decision-making abilities and the trust they earn from the other crew members. No one wants to work with a micromanager; it kills creativity and development. A leader of a crew has to trust his crew.

A common legend from the United States Military Academy at West Point is that in a leadership class, the prospective 2nd Lieutenants are asked to solve a problem. The base commander wants you to raise this flagpole. The cadets then break off into groups where they predictably devise plans, draw blueprints, design lifting apparatus, assign tasks, and then, after an hour, present their plans. Only then do they find out the answer is, "Sergeant, have your men raise this flagpole."

One of the most underrated skills of leadership is **trust.**

The key is building that trust. This is where leadership comes in. How do you train with your crew? How are they prepared? What goals and expectations do you set for them? If you are the type of officer who only comes out of the office when there is a problem, then do not be surprised if the crews come up with their own goals or their own tactics.

Effective leadership involves being present and engaged with your team regularly, not just during crises. By actively participating in daily operations and offering guidance, you can foster a collaborative environment. Setting clear, achievable goals and maintaining open communication are essential strategies for building trust and ensuring everyone aligns with the organization's mission. Active participation shows your team that you are committed to their success and willing to support them in reaching their goals. When leaders are involved in everyday tasks, they better understand the challenges their team faces, which helps in making informed decisions. This hands-on approach also encourages team members to share ideas and concerns openly, reinforcing a culture of mutual respect and trust.

Presence

Leadership will always be a balance. Delegating vs. doing is always going to be a challenge, but no one becomes a leader because it is easy. A good leader must find that balance. They must train with their crew, clearly outline their expectations, and be available to follow up and stay informed about what's happening. The key facet of good leadership in any industry is being present.

I had bosses in the fire service and in other jobs who simply were never present, that is, of course, until they didn't like something you were doing or how you did it. I even once had an officer ask us crew members at a scene why we were deploying units over here rather than there, and why some crews had full turnout gear on and others did not. We, right there on the road, tried to tell him this is the way we have been doing it for a year. He was truly befuddled as to why, and only out of respect for the rank did we not say to his face, "you haven't come out of your office in a year, half the time you're on the phone, you never join us for training, some days you leave in your car to run personal errands, and frankly, it never occurred to me that you cared how we did it."

Being present is taught in many business leadership courses. For some reason, it is still one of the biggest failures I see from people in management. Go to a store, does the manager get out of the office and walk the floor? Does a plant manager get out to the production line? Does a grocery store boss come out and help a cashier bag? In my line of work, does the company officer come out of their room to check on the rescue crew's progress after their last call or review how the rig inventory went?

Far too often in my career, I have seen mistakes happen, whether on a run or in the station. The administration finds out, the chiefs get involved, and the issue rolls downhill. When the station captain is called in, their response is, "It's not my fault, I didn't know this was going on!" A sign of good leadership at the administration level is *not* allowing this as an excuse, and a step further, taking this as direct proof that the officer is to blame due to a failure to lead.

I have heard managers in various industries complain that they hate being a manager because all they do is babysit people and have to fix major problems. The truth is, if you're fixing major problems often, it is because you, as a manager, did not notice them when they were small. If the boss is present and available, and truly supervising and checking up on the work, they should be able to catch problems long before they turn into major problems. When done right, a lot of the corrective action needed from the manager is nothing more than an informal "heads up" to the employee to let them know of a simple mistake or a lapse. Now, if, after a few reminders and talks, the employee still makes the same mistake, then, of course, more corrective action is needed. But if the manager was not present during these mistakes, then he would not have known this employee had a pattern of this. Now the manager can sit the employee down with confidence for more formal action.

No officer can be present at all times, and this is nearly impossible in the fire service. The company officer, either the Lieutenant or the Captain, is not going on all the 911 calls, just the ones their truck is going on. So, when the junior crews go on a basic ambulance run, they are doing it without any direct supervision. The department operates on the trust that its members are skilled and will perform to standard. That trust, however, is built on the presence of the company officer daily. Is the officer making sure they are trained to the standard the city or the medical control board wants? Is the officer making sure they have the equipment and supplies needed? Is the officer following up when they go on a critical call, or even training or reviewing it with the crew afterward? Or does the officer hang out in his private room with his own cable TV and only come out when the lunch and dinner bells ring?

I had an opportunity provided to me that ended up working out in terms of presence. I knew there was a chance I would get in trouble with the higher-ups, but in the moment, it seemed like the right thing to do and meant a lot to me to be present in this instance.

At the beginning of COVID, our department, like the rest of the country, was taking educated guesses on how to proceed and making it up as we went along. Our department's first policy was to limit exposure by keeping the number of people on the scene to a minimum. We usually send an ambulance for a minor medical, but an ambulance *and* a fire engine for more serious calls to have more hands on the scene in case they are needed. Until we had a handle on what COVID was, we limited the engine on the trouble-breathing runs, so I was going on fewer calls with my team, who were in the ambulance that day. This is on top of attempting to have just one of our ambulances be the "COVID" ambulance, which would go first on suspected COVID. As we soon found out, most of the calls were suspected COVID, so this increased our ambulance's call volume a lot at the beginning.

To top all of this off, we tried to segment off the administration staff from the firefighters or paramedics. We encouraged people not to congregate too much together in the same rooms, even though it is impossible when our shifts are twenty-four hours and the fire stations are only so big. The end result of all these new policy orders, segregation, and uncertainty from daily TV news led to stress among the crews. Sadly, they are so stressed that they worry about their safety. It is only human nature to wonder about these things when you are told to keep separate from the office staff and to use a UV light on the ambulance after every call because they did not know if bleach would kill it, and limit time even exercising so as not to be too close to each other.

I could see the stress on some of the crew members' faces, the fatigue of the call volume setting in, and them starting to doubt the efficacy of their personal protective equipment. Now, I would never suggest that the staff, other officers, or crew members did anything wrong. They did the right thing for themselves and their own personal and family health by being cautious and following the department's and the state health department's guidelines. I just wanted to do it differently and was comfortable making my own command decision.

Instead of keeping a separation between myself and the ambulance crews, I went as extreme in the other direction as I could. When I saw the "COVID" ambulance pulling into the station, I got up from wherever I was, helped them back the rig in, and I asked them how the run went, going as far as to put my hand on their shoulder so they would see I was not afraid to touch them, let alone be near them (some people were). I then offered to help with the cleaning, restocking, and decon. This instilled in them the confidence that they can trust their gear and our procedures, and I was willing to demonstrate this by backing it up with my own possible exposure to a respiratory virus.

I even continued that in the middle of the night, not allowing myself a comfortable night's sleep because I wanted to be there every call to welcome the ambulance crew back and let them see that they were safe, taken care of, and I wasn't afraid of them. Now, of course, after a month or two, things quieted down and we got a handle on dealing with a respiratory virus, so it wasn't as if I never slept for two years, but for two months, I wanted the crew to know I was in this with them.

The phrase "We are all in this together" is overused, especially when it comes out of celebrities' or politicians' mouths. A good leader, though, should strive to be there, to be "in this" with their team. In battle, this happens naturally in the military. When a company needs to wade through a stream, walk through a desert, or eat a Meal Ready to Eat, the captain is right there with them. They all live the same experience.

In the fire station and many other industries, however, this takes discipline from a company officer. It is tempting to hang out in your office, watch TV as the crew goes on calls, and demand they make meals that only you like. An officer who people want to work for puts the crew first, and not because it looks good or you read it in a book, but because the officer truly wants to. Because, deep down, they care more about the crew than themselves.

Being present, once again, is the best way to achieve this. On the fireground, being with your partner sends a great message. Lots of officers say, "I won't ask you to do anything that I am not willing to do myself." The officer has to walk this walk, not just talk this talk. It's not easy in a fire; you get hot, then get really wet, and then have to wear the wet gear for the next hour or two as you overhaul the fire and look for extension. In the winter, it's sometimes below freezing where I work, and when your gear gets wet, it also freezes. At an industrial fire, it gets hot, confining, and greasy trying to get near the seat of a machine fire. Is the officer going to be there next to their partner, sweating, freezing, and getting dirty? If you want the crew to follow you, you will.

Navy SEAL and public speaker Jocko Willink says it best: "A leader needs to participate in the suffering."

" Listen carefully to the sound of my voice, because this is the loudest you will ever hear me speak to you.

—*Tony Dungy, NFL coach*
"

4

Making the Transition

If you are going to steal, steal from the best. Coach Dungy would use this phrase when he met with the new members of the team every training camp. I use it as the first words I say at our roll call meeting when we have a rookie join our crew on their first day. I want someone coming into a new job or new department to know right away that the crew will be supportive and welcoming. Most important is for them to know that support will first and foremost come from the top if we are in the station, at a medical scene, or a building fire. I will give orders in a professional voice and tone. If they do something well, I will let them know in front of the crew; if they do something wrong, I will let them know calmly, and more importantly, in confidence in the office. Praise in public, punish in private.

When I was younger, on the job, and even as a part-timer in a prior department, I learned from the occasional bosses who would yell when anything went wrong or just not the way they wanted. All their orders at the fire scene were shouted as if they had to be heard over gunfire in a battle. We just called them "screamers." If someone asked me, How is it working for so and so, I could just say,

"Oh, he is a screamer," and everyone would know what I meant. As I have already said in previous chapters, "I don't want to be that guy."

A calm presence was something I set as a goal for myself years before being promoted to officer. Luckily for me, this is close to my nature, so it came easily. What was harder for me was to have a strong presence. That took work. Knowing the job, of course, is the best way to develop that presence because making sound decisions and having those decisions turn out to be correct is what builds the trust the crew has in your decision-making abilities. After a few 911 scenes that go well, the crew will trust your decisions. If things do not go well, then the crew will base their trust on how you handle it going forward. Will you admit to making a mistake and work at learning from it, or will you deflect and blame the junior guys? The choice is yours.

One thing I learned as a new lieutenant was how knowing the job, being good at the job, and distilling that to making correct decisions on scene not only developed the crew's trust in me but, more importantly, developed my own trust in myself. That, more than any class or certification I had, developed my ability to have confidence in my decisions. The more I trusted myself, the more I was able to speak calmly and with confidence. Most of the "yellers" I have met as managers are yelling because of their own insecurity rather than the mistakes the crew is making.

How does a leader develop that trust in themselves?

As I mentioned earlier, for me, it was about being good at the job and making good decisions on the scene. From day one, I had confidence that I knew what I was doing, that I would still make mistakes and always be learning, but I knew this was a job I could do. That confidence was not bolstered by my superiors, however. It seemed like, for the first few months, I was never making my supervisory chiefs happy, and they were not shy in letting me know about it. Sometimes they were right, sometimes I defended my decision-making to no avail, and sometimes they were just mad I was there. Either way, I sometimes doubted myself and the decisions I had to make. This is no way to lead a crew. I make sure and tell my senior firefighters, if in charge, to make the best decision they can at the time, with the crew or the patient's best interest at heart. I absolutely do not want them to make a decision in the heat of the moment, with someone's safety on the line, based on whether they think they will get in trouble or be yelled at.

This was how I started my transition, sometimes making decisions based on whether I thought the chief would get mad or not. That type of management never leads to good decisions or decisive leaders. I spent many scenes trying to direct my crew or check on how many patients an accident had, or if there were any other hazards, and found myself having a superior in the middle of the scene asking me why I was doing it this way or that way. There is no way to run an emergency scene or develop confidence.

Surely enough, though, I did go on enough calls with my crew, and we made a difference with positive outcomes for the patient or the property owner, so that they started trusting me. I didn't pick up on their level of trust right away, still being distracted by the criticisms of my bosses. I know I should not have let them get in my head, but they did, and it made me hesitant to make decisions.

This changed on one very particular run. My captain was off, so I was on the ladder truck, and the other lieutenant was on the engine. A call comes in for a man stuck on a roof. The caller is unsure if the man is injured, but says he is lying down. After the ambulance and engine were there for ten minutes, they called for the ladder truck I was on as backup. As we were en route, the rescue crew radioed and informed me that the patient was dead on the scene. Now I knew this was not a mere assistance call. When we arrived, I hopped off the rig and proceeded to the backyard. As I got close, I could hear the voices of three junior firefighters sounding agitated, complaining they didn't know what to do because another officer was not making any decisions and was leaving everything to the junior crew on the ambulance to decide. I then heard one of them say, "It will be okay; Lt. Andrew is on the way." The other firefighters said, "Oh, good, it's going to work out."

Now I am not sharing this to fluff up my own ego and sense of self. I am sharing it because, in that moment, I finally realized I was reaching the crew. That my decisions were respected and my leadership was valued. In short, I realized I was doing a good job, that they trusted me, and more importantly, that the jibber jabber from the chiefs was just noise. I just had to keep doing what I was doing and not doubt myself.

Earn that Respect

As mentioned before, the fire service is a paramilitary organization. We're not the military. We don't separate our officers and firefighters; we live, eat, and work together, and we're also real friends off duty. You can't expect the crew to respect you just because you have a bugle on your collar. You have to earn that respect.

There's the rub. Earning it.

I will always keep pounding the drum that being good at the job is a great way to earn respect. But it is only the first step. Whether you are a new or experienced company officer, the next best thing, and possibly just as important, is **leading by example**.

Frustratingly, I still see managers in various fields tell their young workers to "Don't do what I do, kid." This is as effective as telling a teenager not to smoke or drink when you are "That hypocrite who smokes two packs a day." If there is a uniform policy, then follow it. If there is a training class with the crew, then attend it (and participate). If there is a new SOP from the chief, then obey it. It is a common phrase because it is true: actions speak louder than words.

Embody the standards that you expect from the crew. Being punctual, well-trained, working hard, and doing these things when no one is around to see it are things all bosses ask of their crews. It is not that hard to demand that of yourself. Don't be the guy who only participates in training when the chiefs are looking.

Leading by example does not mean you have to do all the work and take the lead on every project, but being involved is still important. If you, as the boss, never attend any training or participate in projects, it's not surprising if the crew views these projects as unimportant. As someone who has taught classes for fire departments, nothing spoils the enthusiasm of the young, impressionable members more than the boss in the back row complaining about how long it is while playing on their phone or talking. If it's not important for the officer to learn, then the younger members will never think it is important for them.

Being an example to others by your presence is certainly important; however, leading by example goes much deeper than that. Many times, the best examples are behaviors or values that you demonstrate every day. The culture you create through your hard work or conduct can inspire your team and, more importantly, inspire them to work hard even when you're not there to supervise. Strive to create a culture where they are motivated to always do their best and work towards a common goal.

A great example of this in the fire service is cleanup after a meal. The goal is that we eat as a crew and even hang out after the meal—we actually call it family time! It is rare, however, that we ever get through a meal without one of our rigs catching a run. Let's say, for example, I am on the ladder with three people. The engine and the ambulance get a call. Then the three of us will do all of the cleanup and dishes while they are on a call. Nothing kills morale more than coming back from a 911 call or two and seeing that the crew "left some work for you."

Now, let's say I am the acting chief for the day. I am in a staff car by myself, and all the rest of the crew leave on runs. I could, as the acting chief, retreat to my office and leave the mess for them when they get back, and no one would complain to me; they would respect the rank and understand I might have administrative duties to do. Or I could get up, load the dishwasher, wash the pots, sweep the floor, and take out the trash. Because in the end, we all live there. It's our house, so why would I want to look at a pile of dishes and trash for an hour or two while they're gone? More importantly, why would I want to leave work for people who are actually working while I don't have anything else to do? Something as simple as doing the dishes in their absence does more to create a culture of caring about the work than any rules or regs. In addition, it shows that having a clean station is not only important, but it is important enough for the boss to care enough to pitch in. If the boss cares, then they will care.

Empathy

A great way to get the crew to care about the mission is for you to care about them. No one wants to work for a boss who is a pushover, but another significant step in earning respect is **showing empathy**.

In the fire service, they are sometimes putting their lives in your hands with your decisions, but many times they are also putting their careers in your hands as well. Their ability to learn on the job, improve, stay safe, have a long career, avoid trouble, and prepare for promotion depends on how leadership molds and supports the workers. Too many times, I have seen young people develop bad attitudes or even burnout from a lack of leadership support. If someone is stressed, the boss should notice it through actual supervision and reach out to that person, rather than letting the stress fester and escalate. This is especially important when a worker makes a mistake or, worse, quits due to the stress.

In every person's career, they will have times when they are dealing with external issues that are distracting them from their work. A good supervisor notices these small changes in behavior. If a normally poor performer is performing poorly, then that deserves some corrective action. If, however, a good worker is suddenly preoccupied and struggling, it should be noticed early. An effective leader can then pull that employee aside and ask (in confidence) what is going on and if there is anything they can do to help. Being an active listener is one of the first steps in showing empathy. Still, it must be followed up with actually understanding what they are going through and acknowledging their feelings. You actually have to demonstrate that you care.

A great example is when a person has a complaint or a suggestion. Sit down with them, listen to their idea, provide feedback, and talk in depth with them about their recommendation. Then take their idea and present it to your bosses. If the idea has merit, maybe it will get adopted. Even if it is not adopted, this becomes something tangible to show the employee that he or she was heard.

Caring about them also includes preventative action. A leader should also lead in training the team. Review policies and procedures, read new policies out loud in a meeting rather than assume the crew will check their email. When technical aspects of the job haven't been used in a while, hold a refresher class. If another crew or team has an issue or a problem, review the lessons learned. While not the technical definition of empathy, this is a very effective way of caring about the crew. It is one of the best ways you can stay safe from danger on the job or from discipline in the office. So many times, I have seen a young person make a mistake on a medical run and find themselves in the chief's office. While the burden of knowing your job rests on you, I've always been disappointed in officers who haven't provided training or reviewed paramedic care and policies, assuming the crew would never forget or know what to do in every situation. Show your team you care by being there and giving them the knowledge to keep them safe.

Do you care if they have long and fruitful careers?

One shocking thing I have seen in various companies and even a few fire departments is a manager so insecure that they stifled or even shut down their workers' ability to improve themselves. Whether preventing them from attending seminars or classes, assigning them to work late if they are working on a degree at night, or not giving them credit on assignments that you are forwarding to your bosses, the worst of the worst leaders think their stature is based on the people they keep down and under them.

To take this a step further, a real leader has no problem if someone they trained is promoted, and promoted again, and even promoted above them. Seeing anyone you trained succeed is a compliment to your training. A good leader actually takes pride in seeing someone they guided succeed. Unfortunately, many managers keep people down to make themselves feel superior.

In reality, the leaders who care the most about their workers not only want them to promote up, but also *help them* promote up. It should be a source of pride as a leader when a promotional list comes out for a competitive position and one of your team members is number one on the list. This not only demonstrates their growth but also reflects positively on your leadership and the supportive environment you foster. Encouraging and facilitating their advancement ultimately strengthens the entire team.

Conversely, if you manage a group of people and after twelve years all of them are still in the same cubicles in the same office doing the same jobs, that is a reflection of your ability to manage people. Encouraging, coaching, and mentoring are common management seminar phrases for a reason. They are all desired qualities in a leader. The key is that the leader needs to coach and mentor, not just to help the employee get better, but to inspire them to make themselves better. This empowerment is what builds a culture of growth. Not only the employee's growth, but also the company's growth. The goal of caring is not just to support the one struggling worker; it is for the entire team to have collective success.

> A ruler should be slow to punish
> and swift to reward.
>
> —*Ovid*

5

Poor Worker or Poor Leader?

When I was young on the job, I had to learn to form my own opinions and follow my instincts. The thing is with the culture of the fire station, we work twenty-four hours in a row. There is one shift a day, and however many stations you have. If someone works on another day and at another station, you might not see that person for years unless you are at the same union or social function. The absence of daily contact with coworkers allows the human nature of gossip and rumor to become perceived as truth. For some, this clouds their opinions of people they might have never worked with. I quickly learned that many work issues were misunderstandings, exaggerations, or flat-out wrong.

What I also came to see after I had some time on the job is that even legitimate mistakes that a person would make many times were a reflection of that crew's leadership. This happens so much that ever since, when I hear of some young firefighter not performing well, I always question how they were taught and how they were led. This does not mean that if someone is showing a pattern of poor performance, they are absolved. It just means I always look to the crew they were on, because more often than not, the bad habits were exactly how they were taught.

If a crew does not do the chores every day, then do not be surprised if your young employees think it's normal to let the trash pile up. If the crew is always complaining about a silly EMS call, then do not be surprised when the new guy complains all the time. If the crew is snotty to the public, then do not be surprised that the new worker also has a bad attitude.

So often when I hear "I hope you don't have to work with Joe, he is terrible," I always ask, Who are the officers or senior firefighters on the crew, and what example are they setting? I've seen the old guys, too many times, dirtbag a young man because their buddy on the other crew said he's a jerk. The thought never crossed their mind to find out for themselves or develop their own opinion. They were completely willing to dislike someone for a whole career (and even give them low promotional scores) because this guy said that this other guy told him what someone else said.

If a poor performer is truly displaying poor attitudes and work habits, and you are sure it's not a reflection of the example they were shown, then you must look at why this worker is struggling. As discussed in the previous chapter, **empathy** should be the first response. Not showing weakness or fear to act, but reaching out to the employee can sometimes uncover an underlying issue that is a distraction, if not the flat-out cause of the problem. Showing the employee you care can go far in building a team and in building their self-esteem. By offering support and understanding, managers can help employees address personal challenges and improve their performance. This approach not only resolves issues but also fosters a positive work environment where employees feel valued and motivated.

More times than I can remember, a worker who had been at a high level was displaying issues of poor performance. Rather than jumping directly to discipline, I was able to have an informal talk. These talks, if kept in confidence, can go a long way to getting people to feel like part of the team and "buy in" to the mission. Specifically, just saying "You haven't been yourself lately, tell me what is going on," or "I know you're better than this" are questions that do more to help a struggling worker than any discipline. It shows them you care, regardless of any recent troubles, that you still believe in them, and you want to help them with their career.

Many times, an employee will open up about a problem at home or with family or even with their health, which explains why they are distracted. You might be able to help them by providing access to Employee Assistance Programs or by having an informal conversation with their peers to reassure them that they're not alone. Sometimes having a senior crew member reach out to him has a two-fold benefit; the employee has a peer that is showing he cares and letting him know that the crew has his back, and it also provides an opportunity for a senior worker, who isn't yet an officer, to work on some leadership skills and gives them the confidence of being trusted by the boss.

To determine if a worker is failing due to poor habits or poor leadership, observe their work patterns and interactions. Poor habits may include procrastination or disorganization, while poor leadership might manifest in a lack of guidance or support. Evaluate whether the worker has access to adequate resources, training, and feedback. If the support systems are lacking, it may indicate a leadership issue rather than a personal shortcoming. Additionally, consider if other team members are experiencing similar challenges, which could further suggest leadership problems. If multiple people on the team are off their game, it is almost always something that can and should be addressed by the officer. It might be simply that the workload is high this month, which cannot be changed, but maybe a different rotation of job assignments can offer a break. Sometimes, a personality conflict arises, and it would be beneficial to give certain members some space and possibly a new assignment. The key is that many things can cause a worker to struggle, but a boss will never know unless they ask the questions and find out.

Once poor habits are identified, offering targeted training and time management workshops can help the worker improve their skills. This is best achieved by setting clear goals and providing regular feedback that can also encourage accountability and better performance. A lot of times, the regular feedback ends up being a form of positive reinforcement that improves the worker's attitude and outlook.

Additionally, pairing the worker with a mentor or coach can offer personalized guidance and support in overcoming these challenges. As discussed in previous chapters, this benefits not only the worker but also the peer acting as a coach to learn their own leadership style. When a senior worker or peer is doing the mentoring, it is more natural for them to have open and honest communication. Even if you are handling the coaching, being open and honest is crucial in addressing performance issues, as it allows for the identification of specific areas needing improvement. The key is that this needs to be a dialogue, so both the worker and officer can express their perspectives, leading to a mutual understanding of the challenges at hand. This collaborative approach fosters a supportive environment where constructive feedback and actionable solutions can be developed.

For any of these mentoring opportunities to work, the leader needs to have built an environment of open communication long before problems arise. Many times, early in my career, I saw people struggle with an issue that not only was overlooked by the boss, but worse than that, they didn't feel comfortable going to the boss because they never thought he would care. We talked about presence in an earlier chapter; some of the best forms of presence are listening. Active listening allows you as a supervisor to provide true, consistent, and constructive feedback. It is impossible to hear anything as a boss if you are holed away in your office.

When the leader is disengaged, it not only creates an atmosphere of distrust but, worse, the leader is not concerned about the team. This lack of leadership not only contributes to low morale but also to a lack of productivity. Without proper supervision, a manager cannot be surprised when the routine tasks around the workplace get forgotten or ignored. This is a killer in the fire service.

At the fire station, we have daily chores involving mopping, surface cleaning, taking out trash, and sweeping up. We live in the station every day, so just like your home, you want to keep it clean. The housework at the fire station serves another purpose; it's a simple task that can be divided among the crew, allowing them to follow orders, work as a team, and complete tasks on time. The same goes for any special project, whether we want to put up a new shelf or assemble some new gym equipment. Simple tasks that show they can work together as a team. The point being, if they cannot handle the simple tasks, how can I expect them to perform at a house fire? This is why the manager needs to be involved; if the manager isn't around to supervise these routine tasks, they cannot be surprised if the building blocks of teamwork are never learned, and then issues of poor performance become predictable leadership failures and not issues of simply a poor worker.

The lesson is that once the crew sees that even the boss is buying into the importance of having a clean station or equipment stocked, it sends the message that having pride in the fire station and the apparatus applies to all of us. This shared commitment fosters a sense of unity and responsibility among the team, ensuring that everyone contributes to maintaining a clean and efficient workspace. Everyone buying in is the best way to eliminate any of your crew from being lulled into bad habits or poor work performance.

When leaders actively participate and demonstrate their commitment, it boosts team morale by fostering a sense of unity and shared responsibility. This involvement encourages team members to take ownership of their roles, knowing their leaders support them. Additionally, it creates a positive work environment where everyone feels valued and motivated to contribute.

The boss being involved and present is the first and best step in figuring out the motivation of a poor worker and truly distilling whether these are issues of inadequate work or poor leadership. When a boss is actively engaged, they can observe firsthand the challenges and dynamics affecting an employee's performance. This involvement allows for more transparent communication and provides opportunities to address any misunderstandings or resource gaps. Additionally, it builds trust and opens up dialogue, encouraging the employee to share their perspective and collaborate on solutions. This also provides opportunities to see issues of poor performance early on so they can be addressed and cut off before they sprout into career-long bad habits.

Millennial or Old Guy

So, who is to blame for poor performance?

Everyone I know who manages people in today's workplace has the same experiences and frustrations. Common phrases I hear are, "These Millennials and Gen Zs are so entitled," or "These kids today don't know how to work hard." But is it their fault, or is it the way they were taught?

Raising kids today has a new set of challenges that have been the topic of an endless number of books on both parenting and psychology. Whether it is internet access, screen time, lack of outside exercise, remote learning, or lack of interpersonal skills, there is no doubt that some of the applicants we are getting have a different background than a generation before. This isn't necessarily a bad thing; the young people today come with a different skill set, which means leaders cannot use only strategies of the past to motivate them.

When we go on medical call, we work as a team of two for simple medical cases and five for patients who are really sick or injured. We need our paramedics to not only work on a team but also sometimes **lead** the team in directing patient care. We hope that after a few months on the job, they will develop enough confidence to take charge of a medical scene and lead the patient care, even up to telling the senior crew members what equipment to grab and what tasks they want done. This does not mean we want a rookie to be bossy, but we need to see if they can properly assess a patient and make the right medical decisions because, soon enough, they will be alone with another rookie and not have senior members there to take over. We need to watch those skills and even confidence develop, so we have to have the trust to send him off on his own, knowing he is ready.

When a new worker comes into the job with nervousness or inhibition, it pushes young workers into the background, where we are not able to assess their skills or experience. These challenges are what make managing people hard. Remember, it's not their fault; it is our job as leaders to work with the people we have and our job to teach, train, and mold them regardless of the challenges.

A great example is that a few years ago, a fellow company officer and I, Jeremy is his name, were discussing motivating younger workers. We both acknowledged that many of our newer employees struggled with shyness and interpersonal relations. Both of us had some young guys who seemed disconnected and quiet, making it hard for the officer to learn about their personality, strengths, and weaknesses and devise a plan for how best to bring out their talents. This officer did something I never thought of, seemed out of the box, garnered some mocking jokes, but…it worked. What he did was put a box on the dinner table and had the crew put their cell phones in it while they were eating. The important thing to know is that the dinner table in the fire station is more than a place to eat. It is the place we gather as a crew, as a team, and even as a family.

Remember, we work 24-hour shifts, are there all day and night, and this socialization is important to make the day not only bearable but even fun. We have the best job in the world, and making friends and being able to hang out with them during downtime is one of the best perks. The dinner table is one of those firehouse traditions where friendships and camaraderie are built. We tell stories, tease each other, tell the cook of the day their food sucks, get to know each other, unwind, and laugh. These traditions play a crucial role in strengthening team bonds and fostering a sense of unity among crew members. Sharing meals and engaging in lighthearted banter create an environment where individuals feel supported and valued, enhancing trust and collaboration. Such activities also help build resilience, as strong relationships can improve morale and make stressful shifts more manageable. This resilience also develops a thicker skin, where that lighthearted banter lets the crew learn to laugh at themselves. This type of fun creates a humility that helps a firefighter deal with the challenge of dealing with a sometimes angry public.

What the officer noticed (by being observant) was that one of his workers never talked and just looked down at his phone while he ate. By asking the crew as a team to put their phones away, he did not single him out, and it eventually allowed him to come out of his shell and develop confidence and better interpersonal relationship skills. This translated into him being more outgoing on the scene, now able to take charge. He was always a sharp paramedic and an excellent worker, but now, because of this officer's keen observation, he became a confident firefighter.

What a heads-up company officer move.

> Effective leadership is putting first things first. Effective management is discipline, carrying it out.
>
> —*Stephen Covey*

6

Poor Worker Is Just a Poor Worker

Fred is struggling on the job. His officer asks him to check the batteries on the heart monitor, log the dates on the IV fluid, and check the air in the SCBA. It does not get done. The officer asks him again and is sure to give clear directions and understand if other tasks come up. It still does not get done. The officer pulls him aside and asks what is wrong to see if there is a distraction that he can help with. Fred just says, "Look, I'm just a fireman, I don't know what you want from me." The officer says I want you to check the batteries on the heart monitor, log the dates on the IV fluid, and check the air in the SCBA. It gets done haphazardly and hours late.

The next day, the officer delegates one of the senior crew members to give him his daily tasks. The senior guy says Can you check the batteries in the heart monitor, log the dates on the IV fluid, and check the air in the SCBA. They don't get done. The senior firefighter, who is more of a peer, asks him why. He answers, "Look, I'm just a fireman, I don't know what you want from me."

The senior guy tells him I want you to check the batteries in the heart monitor, log the dates on the IV fluid, and check the air in the SCBA. Once again, he says, "Look, I don't know what you want from me."

This repeats every day. No matter how simply you asked him to do a task, no matter how clear you made the direction, no matter how understanding you wanted to be, he always acted befuddled, saying, "I just don't know what you want from me."

Sometimes, even with all the new management speak and kinder, gentler leadership styles, the worker is not meeting standards, and it is not because of poor management. Some workers are not working out.

Once the manager can rule out communication issues and confirm that the worker received clear direction, it is now up to the manager to address the problem. In the corporate world or the military, addressing this is usually handled quickly and efficiently, and without sympathy. This is the opposite of the fire service.

As I have mentioned, the firehouse is a home for twenty-four hours, and when things are going well, the crew acts like a family and sometimes like a fraternity. We generally like each other, we are often in the same association or union, and have to work in close quarters for a whole day, sometimes for years. It can be a challenge to discipline because our first instinct is always to give a co-worker a break, be understanding, or even be a friend. There's nothing wrong with that on the surface; however, if, after a few informal warnings and private discussions to rule out issues with home or issues with your communication, you are sure this is the fault of the worker, then strongly addressing it not only helps the performance of the team but also helps the worker themselves.

Many people want to be the boss because they want to be seen as a good guy, and the goal of their decisions is to be liked.

This is death for a leader.

It is, of course, nice to be liked and to have friends. It is good for the team if people get along. But if your decisions are based on whether people will like you or not, you are not helping the crew or the mission. The goal should be to perform at a high level, provide good service, work safely, and ensure that everyone goes home at the end of the shift. The goal should never be to be everyone's buddy.

Even on a one-on-one level, treating someone who is struggling as a friend is not helping them. Ignoring problems and allowing bad habits to continue or become established habits is only hurting them in the long run. If the leader wants to be friends with them, then addressing an issue early truly helps them. It helps them grow and learn from mistakes, and also learn how to take constructive criticism. A strong leader should be able to, without browbeating or yelling, look a worker in the eye and tell them straight. In fact, most workers will respect it.

How you handle coaching or even discipline goes a long way to getting the crew to buy into the goals of the team. If a worker who makes a mistake is berated in public, it only serves to make them hesitant to do their job for fear of being called out. In contrast, if a worker who makes a mistake is taken in private, respectfully talked to, and given clear expectations to improve, it can help crew cohesiveness by showing them they will all be held to a high standard, and if mistakes are made, they will be dealt with respectfully.

A leader who focuses on popularity can lead to compromised decision-making and a lack of accountability. A lot of times, this results in decreased productivity, as important tasks are neglected in favor of maintaining personal relationships. Ultimately, it can undermine team cohesion and the overall success of the mission. It almost always creates riffs in the crew when they see one person making mistakes that are forgiven, especially when they have been called into the office for similar things themselves.

To balance friendliness with professionalism, focus on clear and respectful communication, which fosters a positive atmosphere without compromising on standards. Set boundaries that maintain professionalism while still being approachable and supportive. Encourage teamwork by valuing each member's contributions and ensuring that decisions are made based on the team's objectives rather than personal relationships. By showing the team this respect, you now have a more desirable dynamic than basic friendship.

What if none of this works?

Then it is time to sit someone down and have that hard conversation. Many companies have a set of standard procedures for discipline, and the fire service is no exception. Where we are unique is that many fire departments across the country have a one-year probationary period in which new hires are considered at-will and are closely monitored and evaluated weekly or monthly. If after the year they have performed to standard, then they are now considered regular employees and have full contract or human resources protections. Unfortunately, when I was young on the job, I saw new hires struggle and get passed through. Not because their work warranted it, but because the officers didn't want to be the "bad guy".

This is where the whole system falls apart.

Not only were bad habits allowed to fester and even grow, some workers got worse and when truly egregious errors were made that would result in suspension or termination the administration found their hands tied because all the prior work history that the chief heard about was never documented, so now the employee was able to claim this was a first offense and lesser discipline had to be used. This only allowed the worker to continue to make errors that not only risked a medical patient they were in charge of, but also exposed their partner to the liability of these mistakes. And of course, it just delayed the inevitable when another rule violation or critical mistake happened, the administration now had the paper trail to terminate him. But all of this could have been avoided if the officers had done the hard work of supervising, including coaching, instruction, and evaluating performance honestly, and above all, *documenting* it.

I have seen some extreme examples that went as far as an officer complaining to the chief about a proby's work and overall performance when asked about a critical error in the field or a bad attitude with the public. The conversation goes like this:

"Hey, Cap. How has Fred's performance been? I have a serious complaint here."

"Oh yeah, guy's horrible. Always has a bad attitude and mouths off to superiors and the public."

"Oh, that's odd. I have his evaluations here, and you gave him passing scores each month?"

"Well, you know how it is, you just pencil whip those evals, they don't matter."

In other words, the captain does not want to do their job, wants to be everyone's friend, or, as said before, is just doing it for the money.

This inability to handle the hard conversation of an honest evaluation has two outcomes. The crew will now lack discipline and start to stray or push boundaries themselves because they see poor work not having any consequences. This results in the poor worker continuing to think their behavior is allowed. If allowed to continue, it leads to the worst outcome: a lack of respect for the officer.

Disciplining a Senior Worker

In the fire service, if it's hard to discipline a new worker, it's even harder to take that step with a person who has been on the job for a few years. For all the reasons we discussed in the prior chapter, it is human nature to care enough about people you have worked with for years to give warnings and hope that mistakes are not a pattern. But when discipline is warranted, the boss needs to be strong and step up. The reason for discipline is not to be vindictive; it is to correct the behavior.

If you are in a good organization, you will have procedures for how discipline can be handled. This is a good thing. It provides a boss with the framework for how to use discipline; it also provides the worker with some structure to be reminded that this isn't personal and is being handled fairly.

Many companies give first-level supervisors the authority to give poor grades on a performance evaluation, conduct educational or formal counseling, and sometimes assign extra duties or restrict privileges. These are important, especially the counseling.

Whether in the corporate world or the fire service, it is common to get an email from the administration asking you to read a new memo that outlines a policy. If the policy is important enough, they will include a check box that states that you have read it, or your manager will fill out a training form when the team has read it.

Why do organizations do this? They do it to take counseling away from progressive step discipline. By checking the box, you can no longer say "I didn't know," and now they can go right to playing hardball.

This is good for management; it keeps the ranks on point with policies and procedures. It is not as effective for company-level fire officers or team leaders in the corporate world, as counseling is a very effective way of getting a message across. In the last chapter, we discussed the value in pulling people aside informally and getting to the root cause of poor work. Yet when the root cause of poor work is the worker themselves, having a serious talk with the person, laying out the rules and expectations, and then *writing it down* and sending it through the chain of command is many times effective in jump-starting change in a work habit.

Many managers have studied **Maslow's Hierarchy of Needs**. The first two being Physiological and Safety needs. Counseling does a great job at serving these needs because, unlike informal talks, this is the step that gets the worker to see that if they continue the poor work, they can see the path to being terminated, and like most people, they need the job, the money, and the health insurance.

This "Scared Straight" approach works, and is still a way of disciplining while still maintaining an ability for a struggling employee to turn it around without damage to their future career. As a result, many employees are kept from continuing down the path of worse discipline while being able to learn and still advance within the company.

This approach also fosters a supportive environment where employees feel guided rather than punished, encouraging personal growth and accountability. Addressing issues early helps maintain a positive workplace culture, ensuring that employees can thrive while contributing to the organization's success. On some occasions, more serious discipline is called for; however, if used too early and with a minor infraction, it can lead to an otherwise good worker becoming jaded and bitter.

Before all of this happens, though, addressing performance early is always the better choice. Whether early in a career or as soon as patterns emerge, handling performance issues is necessary, and many times, the worker wants to know how they are doing. The most effective way of doing this is the performance evaluation.

Many companies have monthly evaluations for the first year, and then quarterly after that. The key is being honest. As mentioned before, a real leader would never "pencil whip" the evaluation to avoid looking like the bad guy. But sadly, I have seen a trait that is just as bad.

That is using the evaluation to address issues for the first time. More times than I can count, in my fire career or in the corporate world, I have seen people complain about their performance evaluation, saying this is the first time they have heard these complaints. This is terrible leadership.

For a boss to carry around issues in secret and then sandbag the worker during the eval is unfair and even counter-productive. Worse, it is sometimes vindictive. Too many times, I have wondered if a boss has kept a performance issue private for the sole purpose of keeping someone down. Sometimes it is as if the boss does not want them to improve. I have even heard anecdotes that this tactic is used in the corporate world when they know a downsizing is coming. Whether for vindictiveness or simply laziness on the part of the manager, this is a killer for morale.

Employees will feel demotivated and lose trust in their leadership, leading to decreased productivity and engagement. Without regular and timely feedback, workers are deprived of the opportunity to address and correct their mistakes, which can hinder their professional development. Additionally, this lack of transparency can cultivate a toxic work environment that people do not want to work in.

The evaluation should be a reflection of the regular communication that the boss has with the worker throughout the evaluation period. The boss should be offering daily tips to the worker on how to grow and improve, and at the end of the month, if it is still not getting better, you now have something to really get into during the evaluation process. A good evaluation meeting should always be positive for the worker. Address issues of poor performance and then provide encouragement and steps to take to improve. The worker should leave the evaluation feeling respected enough to receive direct feedback on areas for improvement, without the boss having to sugar-coat it due to fear of their reaction. Most people prefer being looked in the eye and told the truth.

Another benefit to this constructive but direct documenting of areas to improve is that the worker now has a goal to achieve before the next evaluation. Often, these "areas" can be upgraded and documented on the next evaluation, demonstrating to your bosses that your worker was given opportunities to improve and responded by putting in the effort to get better, all without resentment or bitterness. Now the worker has the pride in their own performance to carry them forward. Also, the higher-ups know the worker can handle constructive criticism and is willing to work hard to improve.

Once again, however, what if these tactics don't work?

Then the boss cannot be afraid of running it up the chain of command. Sometimes the performance warrants it, and if the boss cannot pull the trigger on getting it handled, they are only putting the rest of the team and the mission at risk.

Not everyone is suited to harsh discipline up to and including firing someone. Frankly, I am one of them. I knew early on I didn't want to be an administrator; I always wanted to be on the road, doing calls and leading people. Disciplining someone on a crew where everyone gets along is hard, and it becomes even harder when it escalates and could cause someone to lose their career. But that is why the administration is there and why they make the money they do.

Bare Minimum Guy

In workplaces across the globe, I am sure everyone has to deal with someone who does just enough to get by. Some people blame corporations for stagnant pay and a lack of promotions for disincentivizing hard work. In the fire service, though, the promotions open up as you get higher in seniority and usually involve various interviews and exams that give everyone an opportunity, so it is hard to blame a lack of mobility for workers just doing the minimum. Some people are happy just getting along, not motivated by a pay raise, are bitter from a prior lost promotion, but many times, they are simply not highly motivated people.

Dealing with a lack of motivation is as difficult as dealing with true substandard performance. Sometimes a boss can see if there is a personal issue bothering the worker or some other personal conflict on the crew. The boss can find opportunities to work or train together as a crew, and maybe some camaraderie will develop for the person to work harder for the sake of solidarity. If appropriate, the team can bring some fun or even competition to the work. With many people, however, this will not work. Deep down, they are just not very driven.

What is the leader to do?

It depends on whether the mediocre guy is not performing to standard or is actually deficient in their job description. Any of the counseling or discipline we discussed is on the table. Yet, what if they are doing their job, even though not going above and beyond?

Whether in a fire department or a corporation, a worker can be reminded that effort and motivation are traits that can be used to qualify a person for promotion, and hopefully, these opportunities for professional development can boost motivation. There are some people, though, who just don't care. I have worked with several people who, if the chips were down, knew how to do their job. Not only that, sometimes they were even good at it. I have also had workers who would do anything I ask and do it on time and at least proficiently. But if I don't ask them to do anything, they will do nothing.

In the fire service, there is only so much training, paperwork, and chores you can do when there is not a 911 call coming in. There is built into the day some needed downtime. No one wants to exhaust your crew all day and then see them run out of gas at 3 a.m. after their fourth medical run of the night. There is nothing wrong with pacing yourself and having some downtime. All the crew members have to come in and check off their equipment and rig for the day first thing. When the mandatory work is done, then, barring any training, they are encouraged to take a break. There is a difference, however, between a break and watching TV all day.

Once again, if there are jobs that need to get done, the leader should have no problem assigning them and having those orders carried out. Yet, if the boss has to be the one noticing the work needed and has to assign every little detail, then motivation needs to be addressed. Fortunately, most people who come to work are motivated and follow through, doing a great job. But back to the original question, what if a worker is doing just enough?

It might be counterintuitive, but if the worker is not violating any rules and their only issue is not being a go-getter, then *let it go.*

If after trying team building, possible pay raises, and encouragement, nothing works. Let it go. More than likely, you are not dealing with an issue related to the organization but rather a lack of motivation that is more an issue of their deep-seated personality than an issue with your leadership. The question then becomes, how long do you want to spend trying to completely change a person's entire personality?

The reality is that at this stage in life, you probably won't. All you will do is try for months or years, and probably fail, all the while ignoring the members of the crew who do want to do more, and with guidance can achieve greatness. If someone does the bare minimum, then let the others be the go-getters and let them be mediocre. There is only so much you can do.

As we consider the path of leadership in the fire service, one of the pivotal questions emerges: How committed are you to becoming the best version of yourself in this role? It's not merely about showing up; it's about actively engaging with the responsibilities and challenges that come with the job. Are you dedicating time to deepen your knowledge through textbooks and trade magazines? Are you taking the initiative to sign up for classes or seminars designed to sharpen your skills? Staying informed about the latest techniques and tools is essential, yet it requires a proactive mindset. Alternatively, is the temptation to coast through the week appealing? Do you find it easier to blend into the background, avoiding the effort of going above and beyond while hoping your job remains uneventful?

Mediocrity can creep into any profession, and the fire service is no exception. It's not uncommon for individuals to experience a decline in motivation at various points in their careers. There are often complex reasons behind this phenomenon. Factors such as personal circumstances, burnout, or even internal department politics can sap enthusiasm. For some, the allure of doing the bare minimum—just enough to maintain their position without facing disciplinary action—becomes a comfortable routine.

Sometimes it is not all their fault when poor leadership siphons their enthusiasm with years of bureaucracy. While poor leadership can certainly foster such an environment, it can also create a cycle where those who lack drive find themselves in positions of authority, motivated more by financial gain or the prestige of the title than by a true passion for the work.

Throughout my career, I've witnessed various firefighters and paramedics grappling with motivation and, as a result, job performance. These individuals can appear to be just going through the motions, lacking the spark that drives true excellence in our field. I distinctly recall an incident involving a firefighter who struggled to effectively handle certain tools during an emergency response. We organized a training session afterward, hopeful that it would spark some newfound interest. However, I quickly observed that once our session concluded, he returned to the recliner, where he spent far too much of his day— idealizing a role rather than embodying the commitments that come with it.

Rather than allowing frustration to set in regarding our challenges in motivating him, I chose to step back and reflect on the broader context of his career journey. I began to compare his situation with that of other firefighter-paramedics I have known over time. This introspection revealed a crucial point: We are indeed fortunate that a significant number of individuals enter this profession out of a genuine desire to help others in need. Their call to service often outweighs their personal ambitions. Others are comfortable just coasting.

The difference in motivation levels between these groups highlights a critical need for leadership in the fire service that not only nurtures skills but also inspires passion. We must remember that each individual comes with a unique background, experiences, and personal motivations. As future leaders, we have a responsibility to cultivate an environment that promotes not just competence but a collective commitment to excellence, ensuring that every member of the team is engaged, motivated, and dedicated to the noble cause of service. In doing so, we can break the cycle of mediocrity and create a fire service that not only meets the expectations of the community but exceeds them.

Luckily, most people become firefighters because they enjoy helping people. Sadly, others become firefighters so they can tell girls at the bar they are firefighters.

"
The nation will find it very hard
to look up to the leaders who are keeping
their ears to the ground.

—*Sir Winston Churchill*
"

7

A Confident Leader

If you have put the work in and are lucky, the crew will buy into the team's mission and work together as a cohesive unit. When it comes to leadership, how does a leader go about it on a daily basis?

The key is not to change what you have been doing that helped build that cohesiveness. Continue with your communication, empathy, and support. But more important than that, a good leader needs to have the confidence to trust themselves to maintain their plan for managing the crew.

Leading with confidence is essential. When leaders exude confidence, they inspire trust and respect among their team members, which can lead to increased morale and productivity. Confidence allows leaders to make decisive choices and navigate challenges effectively, setting a positive example for others. Moreover, confident leaders are more likely to foster an environment where team members feel empowered to share ideas and take initiative.

We previously discussed empowering crew members to handle projects and manage junior people. This needs to continue with how comfortable they are in sharing their ideas with the boss. If a leader shows confidence, this is what makes team members comfortable in bringing their ideas forward. A lack of confidence, or even worse, real insecurity, is a killer to the crew if you want them to grow on the job. Nothing is worse than a senior member who gathers the courage to make a suggestion and only has it shouted down and ridiculed by a manager who feels threatened.

Not only have I experienced this firsthand at the fire station, but I have also witnessed it on a fireground. A young firefighter notices something and says something and even makes a suggestion to the incident commander, only to have this chief say, "Oh, I see, so you think you're in charge. Who do you think you are? You see this badge?!"

Of course, this is unprofessional and a detriment to morale. Yet more than that, it is a real-time demonstration of this chief's lack of confidence and complete insecurity in their own fireground knowledge and decision-making. For me and my peers, coming up the ranks, it was also a demonstration of what not to do.

Hoover, from the aircraft safety YouTube channel "Pilot Debrief," says it is best when discussing flying errors that led to a crash, "There is no room in the cockpit for arrogance."

In fact, the best way to show confidence is not only to listen to the crew's ideas, but to actually ask them what they think. I always do this at a fire or a trauma victim:

ask the team on a medical or my partner at a fire what they think.

A simple, "Hey Joe, looks like heavy smoke on the second floor, what are you seeing?"

Or, "I think the hypoxia is causing this bradycardia, I'll manage the airway and respiration first unless someone sees anything else."

"Yeah, Cap. I saw he was on a beta blocker; I want to get a 12-lead EKG right away in case it's a heart block."

"Hey, great idea."

These on-scene discussions go a long way to show the crew that you trust their experience and judgement and show them they are valued. It also shows the crew that you have the confidence in yourself to want to listen to other ideas without being married to yours.

This confidence also carries to the station. You must feel comfortable delegating tasks to the senior members. Giving them the trust and the authority to manage tasks and people not only develops their decision-making, but also reinforces to the entire crew to trust in the chain of command. The boss doesn't *need* to get involved in every matter or decision in a workplace. And more importantly, they should not *want* to.

A leader who wants to make every decision only does so because they either do not trust the crew or do not trust themselves. In most cases, I've found that giving the crew space to work on their own often impresses me with their ingenuity in finding solutions.

We discussed the first two of Maslow's Hierarchy of Needs; however, if handled right and done consistently, it can fulfill the next three on the list: Belonging, Esteem, and Self-Actualization.

When a leader is confident enough in his crew to handle both low-level situations as well as important tasks such as training and having a voice in the tactics used to accomplish a mission, his team will naturally feel like they belong and that they are making a real contribution.

Empowerment in leadership involves trusting team members to make decisions. When this is done, it organically helps the crew take ownership of their roles. This approach not only boosts morale but also encourages innovation and accountability. When team members feel empowered, they are more likely to take initiative and strive for excellence in their work. Empowerment with true trust in a team member actually has the possibility to prevent the laziness discussed in the prior chapter.

Leading with confidence should be part of a leader's daily routine. This doesn't mean, however, that it should ever be ok for a leader to be arrogant (No pointing at your badge). Yet when done every day, it sets a tone.

"I've Seen it All, Kid"

We talked about being good at the job as one of the best ways to develop leadership skills. What, however, do you do when you are now in a leadership role? Simple, never stop learning, and always let the crew see you willing to learn. That humbleness shows the crew right in front of their eyes that if the boss has room to improve, then they do as well.

Telling the new-hire you "have done it all" never works. One, you want to have your team always be willing to learn, and two, it is simply not true. No one has seen it all; there is always a 911 call to go on that you have not seen before. This, on top of the world and its technology constantly changing, a good officer knows that they will always come across new things. Showing the team that you have an open mind to learning sets a tone. If the leader wants to learn or sharpen a skill, the crew will follow and want to sharpen theirs.

When the team chooses to follow, that is the first step in leading.

The traditional leadership model, often romanticized in movies and TV and ingrained in many organizational structures, paints a picture of the leader as an omniscient figure—a fountain of knowledge and unwavering authority. This image, however, is a dangerous myth, particularly in the high-stakes environment of the fire service or even modern business. The reality is far more nuanced. Expecting a leader to possess all the answers, to possess perfect foresight in every situation, is not only unrealistic but actively detrimental to effective team performance and overall organizational health. As mentioned before, this "all-knowing" leader often fosters an environment of fear and stifled creativity, where subordinates hesitate to voice concerns or offer alternative solutions, fearing reprisal for perceived inadequacy or challenging the established authority.

Consider a scenario: a Fire Lieutenant, steeped in years of experience, rigidly adheres to a single tactical plan, despite emerging evidence suggesting its ineffectiveness in the current situation. This inflexibility, born from a belief in his own absolute competence, can lead to disastrous outcomes, jeopardizing both the mission and the lives of his team. Conversely, a leader who embraces a "leading by learning" approach would not only solicit input from his team but also actually adapt the plan based on new information and foster a culture of collaboration and shared responsibility. The willingness to adjust strategy based on evolving circumstances is not a sign of weakness but a testament to adaptability and strategic thinking.

In the fire service, we tell our young members, if what you're doing isn't working, then change your tactics. The boss must be willing to do the same.

This isn't to say that experience and expertise are irrelevant. Seasoned public safety professionals undoubtedly possess invaluable knowledge and skills. A true leader, though, will not hoard this knowledge but strategically deploy it and leverage it to foster growth and collaboration within the team. The rigidity of the traditional paramilitary model stifles the potential contributions of every member of the team. Every individual on a team brings a unique perspective, a distinct skillset, and a fresh viewpoint to a situation. Even in the military, the drill instructor/recruit dynamic is not how a company operates once outside of basic training.

By creating an environment where these voices are not only heard but actively sought out, a leader harnesses the collective intelligence of the entire team, leading to better decision-making and a greater chance of success. Simply put, a learning-oriented leadership style is also a confident leadership style.

The benefits extend beyond immediate operational effectiveness. A learning-oriented leadership style dramatically improves team morale and job satisfaction. When team members feel valued, empowered to contribute their ideas, and see their leader as a fellow learner, a stronger sense of camaraderie and trust develops. This heightened sense of belonging reduces stress and increases resilience, particularly crucial in the demanding world of firefighting or modern business, where individuals routinely face high levels of pressure or even danger. The traditional, top-down approach, on the other hand, often fosters a climate of distrust, resentment, and burnout.

Various books have been written about management, and studies have been conducted on team cohesion and individual psychological well-being within various high-pressure environments. Numerous studies have demonstrated a strong correlation between a learning-oriented leadership style and improved team morale, decreased rates of burnout, and increased job satisfaction. These findings underscore the importance of shifting away from the outdated notion of the all-knowing leader toward a model that values collaboration, open communication, and continuous learning. The data clearly support the notion that leadership isn't about having all the answers; it's about creating an environment where everyone can learn, contribute, and grow.

This shift requires a fundamental change in leadership philosophy. Leaders must actively cultivate a culture that embraces mistakes as learning opportunities, fosters open communication about failures, and actively encourages continuous professional development. This involves creating opportunities for training, mentorship, and feedback, establishing clear channels for communication, and ensuring that all team members feel safe to express their concerns and share their ideas without fear of reprisal. It also involves modeling this behavior oneself: openly admitting when a leader doesn't know the answer, actively seeking out diverse perspectives, and demonstrating a commitment to lifelong learning.

In the fire station, a common way we get a younger worker to either gain confidence or buy into our training is to have them study a task, tool, or even a medical treatment and present it to the crew as the instructor. They now see we are willing to listen to them and value their opinion, and we trust their opinion. They also deeply learn that information themselves because they need to truly understand it to be able to teach it. This is walking the walk when it comes to valuing your team, when you can sit and learn from them.

The transition from the mythical all-knowing leader to a leader who embraces continuous learning is not merely a matter of adopting new techniques or methodologies. For a lot of new officers, it's a profound shift in mindset and a commitment to fostering a culture of growth and development at every level of the organization. Often, it's a shift in perspective due to how they were taught as they progressed through the ranks. But by abandoning the outdated and unrealistic expectation that leaders must have all the answers, and embracing a model that prioritizes collaboration, adaptability, and continuous learning, first responders, and indeed organizations in any high-pressure environment, can enhance operational effectiveness, improve team morale, and create a more resilient and adaptable workforce better equipped to navigate the challenges of a constantly evolving world. The path to effective leadership is not about possessing all the answers, but about the continuous pursuit of the answers.

The previous discussion highlighted the detrimental effects of the "all-knowing leader" myth, emphasizing the necessity of a leadership style that prioritizes continuous learning and adaptation. Building upon this foundation, I hope to delve into the crucial role of vulnerability and openness in cultivating a truly effective and collaborative team environment. This isn't simply about being "nice" or "approachable;" it's about strategically employing vulnerability as a leadership tool to foster trust, enhance communication, and unlock the collective intelligence of the team. For me, being "nice" or "approachable" came easily as it is part of my natural personality. Learning how to strategically employ it took work as an officer.

A leader's willingness to admit uncertainty, to acknowledge mistakes, and to openly solicit feedback creates a profound shift in team dynamics. In the high-stakes world of public safety, where decisions often carry life-or-death consequences, the perceived infallibility of a leader can be paralyzing. Team members may hesitate to question decisions, even if they harbor serious doubts, fearing retribution for challenging the authority figure. This silence can be catastrophic, suppressing valuable insights and potentially leading to flawed strategies and dangerous outcomes. Not just different viewpoints, but in firefighting or paramedicine, actual different views.

On the fireground, a junior firefighter might actually see something in the building construction or the smoke pattern that I did not see from my angle. When making a tactical plan, I need that information to develop the right strategy. I will walk around the building to get a 360-degree view, but if I miss something or conditions change, and the crew is afraid to tell me, it is not going to end well for anyone.

One example that sticks with me is in a larger fire department like the one I work at, the staffing is dynamic. Depending on how many people are off on vacation, sick, or injured, our daily staffing can change at the various stations. To deal with this, the battalion chief at our main station calls the outer stations every morning at the start of the day to tell us how many people we will have, whether we are getting anyone detailed in from another station, or whether we are detailing one of our people out to another station.

The chief would often instruct us to send someone to another firehouse because they were short-staffed, which resulted in a number that required a fire truck to be taken out of service. Assuming the chief knew this and was going to call back with further instructions later, we carried out the order and sent the guy. A 911 call comes in, and we send the ambulance, but not the fire engine. The chief would call back and say,

"Why is your engine out of service?"

I would say, "Because we only have seven people."

"No, you have eight."

Me: "No, Joe is on funeral leave, we have seven."

Chief: "Well, why didn't you tell me that?"

Me: "Well, um…um…I assumed you knew and would call back with another move later."

This, of course, is a lie. The real reason I didn't correct him was last week when he gave us the staffing and I questioned the order he gave, he blew his stack yelling about how I "don't know how to do his job," and "How dare I question him."

When I am in that position now, and have to call the other stations to set up staffing, it is under the standing order that they always feel free to question my math of the overall staffing because I know, even though we try, sometimes information gets lost, papers don't get forwarded, calendars don't get updated and I might not have the right data. I need them to confirm with me the information, and we can discuss the plan for the day together.

When a leader admits they don't know the answer, it fosters a safe environment for the crew to voice concerns, share alternative perspectives, and even admit their own mistakes without fear of judgment or punishment. This open acknowledgment of fallibility doesn't diminish the leader's authority; rather, it strengthens it by building trust and fostering a sense of shared responsibility. Team members are more likely to engage fully and contribute their best work when they feel safe to do so, knowing that their mistakes will be viewed as learning opportunities rather than sources of condemnation.

In the office, on the fireground, in a medical scene, in training, or on the battlefield, a leader needs to listen to their people. The leader cannot know it all, and more than that, the crew is almost always very smart and has a lot to offer, but only if you let them.

I'll quote Jocko Willink again: "Leadership starts with following."

> Effective leadership is not about making speeches or being liked; leadership is defined by results not attributes.
>
> —*Peter Drucker*

8

Modern Management at the Firehouse?

I spent my career at the Dearborn Fire Department in Dearborn, Michigan. For those who do not know, it is the city where the Ford Motor Company was founded and is currently headquartered. Not only is it their hub of management, it also houses the largest auto factory in their portfolio and, at one time, the largest in the world, the Ford Rouge Plant.

Because of this, many of our views on business are filtered through the view of the auto industry. This industry, like many, underwent significant changes in the last few decades, with one of the most notable being the emergence of what some termed "new management theory." Basically, a number of management styles came about in the 1980s and 1990s that valued the workers and tried to get away from managing people with the heavy hand of intimidation.

These early-century management styles were pervasive in the manufacturing sector from the beginning of the century all the way through the 1980s. These management styles, though, were responsible for the surpassing of the American auto companies in quality and sales by the Japanese makers by the 1990s. Living in an auto town, I grew up around people who worked in factories, hated their jobs, but couldn't leave because the pay and benefits were too good. This only led to workers doing the minimum or, worse, doing poor work. This apathy, however, came from the top down. It was the companies that valued production over quality. Plant managers were told to always keep the line moving regardless of any errors or mistakes. The thought was that it would always get caught later, or the customer wouldn't care. Even worse, the thought that the customer wouldn't dare buy a foreign model.

Yet by 1985, the Honda Accord was the bestselling car in America. I recall some in the auto industry saying it was an unachievable pipedream to warranty a car for 100,000 miles, while in 1980, some manufacturers only covered a year or 12,000 miles. Yet 100,000 is just what Honda and Toyota did.

The auto industry, to its credit, responded by reworking plants to allow more teamwork, valuing employees' opinions, or valuing quality over quantity. As new management slowly crept into Detroit manufacturing, these theories became popular in management classes and textbooks, and yes, even into fire academies and officer training programs. We all had to read Continuous Improvement, Contingency Management Theory, and Quantitative Management Theory. Some of these management theories came and went, others were adopted, and others were tried but didn't fit.

There were four, however, that I have found through over twenty years of being a line firefighter and company officer that were actually true in real life and provided a context for how to manage people in a modern workforce. Those are: Maslow's Hierarchy of Needs, McGregor's Theory X and Y, Total Quality Management, and pretty much anything Peter Drucker wrote.

Maslow

I have already mentioned Maslow twice, but it really does work when developing a strategy for finding what motivates people at various stages of their careers. In fact, the five levels of hierarchy are the underlying tone of many of the examples I have used thus far.

Take a new hire, for example; back in the day, all of our new hires were young men who wanted to be firefighter-paramedics and went to trade schools and fire academies and then worked at small volunteer departments or private ambulance services for a few years, gaining experience before being hired. Many others served four years in the military and earned certifications; they could also use the GI Bill to enter a fire academy and secure a job. Either way, a municipal fire department pays way more in salary and benefits than these two people ever made before. For these people, safety, security, food, and shelter are great motivators. To put it simply, they want to own a home, raise a family, and put food on the table. They will work hard not to lose that, at least for a few years.

Now, however, we in the fire service are seeing people apply who are changing careers to be here or leaving another professional department to come to ours. Many are even taking pay cuts in the short term to make this happen. Why? Because they want to work at a place with either more security and pay later in the career, or they want to feel valued and are not getting that in their previous work. Now, we have new hires who need support that mirrors a worker with fifteen years of experience: growth, fulfillment, and realizing their potential.

In fact, way back in the day, a boss in the fire service, without knowing it, never progressed past seeing an employee as someone who cannot leave because they need the money, hence the management through browbeating and intimidation. Today, if I don't, as an officer, meet their needs, they will have no problem finding another job that will. The fire service today hires people with a diverse set of skills, and the money does not trap them.

X & Y

The common joke of old management is "If we want your opinion, we'll beat it out of you." An exaggeration, but certainly a view of workers as Theory X. The view says workers are unmotivated, avoid work, lack discipline, and need centralized management to control them. In my experience, Theory X people are an extreme rarity. Nearly every firefighter or paramedic I have worked with is Theory Y, which says workers are self-motivated, enjoy their work, and want to take ownership of it. Most workers enter a career job motivated by achieving security, yet as they gain experience and earn seniority, they become less driven by just the money. They want to be fulfilled and feel like they make a difference.

This transformation of workers being more Theory Y highlights the essential role of supportive management practices, which foster an environment where employees can thrive. By recognizing and nurturing the motivations of Theory Y workers, organizations can create a culture of engagement and dedication, ultimately leading to better outcomes for both employees and the communities they serve.

Total Quality Management

Total Quality Management, also adapted later into The Toyota Way, feeds directly into how we manage teams in the fire service. A good company officer will always try to improve, will always involve their team, and focus on meeting the needs of the customer. That last item, the customer, was a new development in the fire service in the 1990s. Previously, taxpayers were often taken for granted, believing that no one could fight city hall and that, as taxpayers, they had nowhere else to turn for service. As we entered the internet age, the public found ways to be heard if not happy about their government, and as fires became fewer and medical calls, in many departments, sometimes tripled, we needed to provide the best service possible, or the residents would find someone who would.

In 1996, Phoenix Fire Chief Alan Brunacini wrote a book aptly titled *Essentials in Fire Department Customer Service.* It angered the old guard because it rethought how to look at the citizens we serve, yet it made some very good points and was at the forefront of changing the way modern fire departments provide their service. We, for the first time, saw our residents, yes, as taxpayers who contribute to our salary, but also as customers who will take their residency elsewhere or even use another service if we don't meet their needs.

Over the last twenty-five years, it has become common in fire departments to see a crew on a medical run for a senior who lives alone, reach out to social services, and follow up with them to make sure they get the food they need. I have even seen some crews cook a meal for a senior and drop it off in the fire truck. Sometimes, when the crews are inside working on and transporting a medical patient, the engine crew can stay after and shovel the snow on the person's sidewalk and porch. If there were a fire, taking the time to cover some valuables or heirlooms and even removing them from the house, and presenting them to the owner as they watch in sadness from the neighbor's porch. This shows the residents that they matter.

Fire departments across the country have also, in the last thirty years, increased their medical licensure from basic care to advanced life support paramedics, now providing the highest level of pre-hospital care to their residents. They also diversified the fire engines to be able to respond to hazardous material, high-angle, and confined space incidents. This continuous improvement is the best way to make an argument to your residents for why your department deserves their tax dollars.

The commitment to continuous improvement within fire departments is crucial for gaining the trust and support of the community. By providing high-quality emergency medical care and diversifying their response capabilities, fire departments can make a compelling case to residents about the importance of funding. Highlighting these advancements not only showcases the dedication of fire-fighters and paramedics but also helps reassure the community that their tax dollars are being utilized to enhance safety and well-being. This transparency and account-ability are vital for fostering strong community relations and ensuring residents feel confident in supporting their local fire services.

Unlike a business, we do not have shareholders, but we do have stakeholders.

Management By Objectives

Peter Drucker started writing about management in the 1960s. The fire service, like many other industries, didn't begin adapting philosophies like his until the 1990s. Now, without even knowing the history of the concept, many fire departments utilize these ideas as part of their daily routine. It is common in a fire company to lead a team by establishing specific and measurable goals early on and having the entire team work together to achieve them. Fire crews that succeed usually decentralize their command, allowing delegation of tasks and involvement of the whole team. One of the biggest developments in my time in the fire service is the investment in employee training. Whether official certification classes at local colleges, seminars, or national academy-level advanced training, firefighters today have access to improve themselves.

This commitment to continuous learning is encouraged, enabling firefighters to enhance their skills and knowledge base. As individuals grow in their expertise, the entire team benefits, leading to improved operational efficiency and effectiveness in emergency responses. Beyond just tactical skills, this investment in training fosters a culture of professionalism and accountability within fire departments. The emphasis on personal and professional growth creates a more proficient and motivated workforce, which is crucial in high-stakes situations where teamwork and quick decision-making can be the difference between life and death.

Management by Objectives aims to improve organizational performance by clearly defining objectives that are agreed upon by both management and employees. This approach encourages participation and communication, as it involves setting specific, measurable goals with a defined time frame and aligning them with the team's overall mission. Through regular reviews and feedback, MBO ensures that everyone is working towards common goals, enhancing motivation and accountability. What I have learned the most in working for a municipal government and a large fire department is that communication is key. Setting objectives is a practical, almost hands-on way of communicating.

The essence of MBO is in its structure, specifically the objectives and the time frame. This not only provides clear direction but also allows the team to better understand the priorities. Doing this can engage the workers in the goal-setting process and, many times, creates that sense of ownership we discussed in the prior chapter. MBO, if applied fairly, allows the workers to feel their contributions are meaningful.

Management As a Tool

Another critical component is the recognition and reward system. Acknowledging hard work and accomplishments, whether through verbal praise or formal incentives, can significantly increase motivation. Employees are more likely to perform at their best when they know their efforts are appreciated. Many managers do not have the ability alone to pass out major rewards like pay raises and promotions, but many times, simple recognition is motivation enough. Knowing your work is appreciated, even if the reward is simply being noticed, touches on all of these modern management theories.

Moreover, modern management emphasizes the importance of flexibility and adaptability. By recognizing that each employee has unique needs and preferences, managers can tailor their approaches to suit individual motivations and work styles. This personalized management strategy not only enhances productivity but also promotes a positive workplace culture.

Another benefit of these modern techniques is that they can inspire the team to remain motivated and dedicated to the work at all times. This ultimately leads to the overall organization's success.

As fire service organizations continue to evolve, the integration of these modern management practices and commitment to ongoing training will undoubtedly play a pivotal role in shaping their future success. A good officer will utilize all these tools in the toolbox to empower their team.

"
A good leader is a person who takes
a little more than his share of the blame
and a little less than his share of the credit.

—*John Maxwell*
"

9

Take from the Good

We have spent a lot of time discussing examples of poor leadership and things not to do when trying to manage people. I have plenty of examples of good leadership traits that I have learned from as well.

When I first started, I had a boss who was a solid fire officer, really knew the job, and cared about the crew. He was loud but one of those "bark worse than his bite" types. I, as the rookie, would always be working hard and "yes, sir" -ing all day to avoid that loud bark. I took that as far as when it was meal time, allowing the senior members and the company officer ahead of me in the line to grab our meals. They didn't seem to notice, and I, of course, was just happy to have a career job, so I was glad to do it. This was followed by me eating fast to be the first one done, so I could be the first up to start washing dishes. As a rookie in a fire department, initiative is one of the most desirable skills we judge them on.

The problem is that if you eat fast all the time, you can still be hungry, not eat a balanced meal, or even end up with a stomachache. Once again, I was glad to do it and didn't think anything of it, nor did the crew, because it was the way they did it.

Fast forward a year, and I get transferred to a new crew, but I'm still the junior guy. My new Captain, like many of that era, was a Vietnam vet. His time in the service influenced many of his decisions and traits, and I saw one of them on my first day. They announce dinner is ready, so I head to the kitchen and stand in line, noticing my new Captain behind me. I apologize and say;

"Sorry, Cap, I didn't see you there. Please go ahead."

"Don't worry, you go first."

"Not at all, sir, please, go ahead of me."

"No, the men eat first."

And there he stood, every meal, every day, and grabbed his plate of food after everyone else got theirs. I remember that moment like it was yesterday, and I recall feeling different as a young member of the department, as if I was valued just a little bit more. I also knew if I were ever a boss, I would do the same. I eat last for a few reasons, the most important of which is that the junior members work way harder than the senior members. They are on the busier ambulance more and busier during the day with chores or projects, so this, to me, is showing them a form of respect for the work they have done and that they deserve to eat first. Another is more practical. In a fire station, we pay for our own meals, go to the market every day, and attempt to cook lunch and dinner. (This, of course, doesn't happen all the time, and many days we are just gone on back-to-back runs all day and have carryout, but we try.) Given the dynamics of shopping, cooking, and sometimes having flexible staffing, it's always possible we won't have enough food. On the rare occasions this happens, I, as the company officer, will go without, not the crew. Ever.

Even though this boss wasn't perfect and had other traits I would look past, I remembered this one and made sure to copy it. In fact, I worked with two other former military combat veterans, one a company officer and the other a staff officer, who did the same at meal time, and it always stuck with me the effect this had on the crew. Not that my first crew and officer were mean or unfair, just that this was how they were taught, and it probably never occurred to them. I felt it was more a lost opportunity than any actual malice.

Author and motivational speaker Simon Sinek believes so much in this leadership theory that he wrote an entire book on it titled *Leaders Eat Last*. One of my favorite quotes from it is: "You can easily judge the character of a man by how he treats those who can do nothing for him."

These were officers who had already made it to their highest ranks and didn't need my help or my influence. They just actually cared that the crew was fed and taken care of before themselves. Simple as that. It changed how I saw the dynamic of a crew in a firehouse and caused me to pay more attention to the traits of people I worked with and make those mental notes of what worked and what did not.

For example, the first officer I worked with, while not part of the "Eat Last" mindset, did have a trait I noticed and have copied. We work for twenty-four hours in a row. The on-coming crew usually shows up twenty minutes early, so there is time for a change of people on the rigs and to get updates from the off-going crew. It also provides an opportunity for the outgoing crew to go home on time if a late call comes in because the on-coming crew can take the call for you. An average medical transport run takes an hour, so if a call comes in a half-hour before shift change, you will probably be stuck late for about thirty minutes as well. No big deal, just part of being a firefighter or paramedic.

My first officer would hang out in the kitchen with the on-coming crew if the ambulance crew got a late run, until the ambulance got back. When asked why he was there, he would say, "I go home when everyone goes home."

This was unique; many officers didn't even notice the ambulance crew was gone, let alone care. I always respected my first officer for doing that and have stolen it for myself. If the ambulance crew is on a late run, I hang out however long it takes for them to get back, meet them at the rig as they pull in, and ask them how the call went before I head to the parking lot.

I didn't realize it for a few years, but I was subconsciously compiling a list of traits like this that I enjoyed and would implement if I had a chance to become a company officer.

Over the years, I've come to recognize that my experiences in various roles and organizations have led me to mentally compile these lists of leadership traits that resonate with me. At first, I didn't even realize I was doing it; it was more of an intuitive process, shaped by the leaders I admired and the environments I thrived in. As I observed different leadership styles, I noted the qualities that inspired me and the ones that didn't quite sit right.

For instance, I found that transparent communication helped me trust and collaborate within a team, while a lack of it can lead to misunderstandings and disengagement. I admired leaders who were empathetic and genuinely listened to their team members, understanding that recognition and validation play a crucial role in motivating individuals to perform their best. I recall the first time a shift battalion chief asked me about a class I took and if I could share any insights I gained that could benefit the department. Sadly, I had four years before that first time an officer cared that I went to a class.

I also noted the importance of adaptability. The most effective leaders I encountered were those who could pivot their strategies in response to changing circumstances, demonstrating resilience and creativity (or, as they say in the military, Adapt and Overcome). The fire service is known for its traditions and resistance to indiscriminate change. Yet the good officers encouraged innovation and were open to new ideas, creating a culture where everyone felt empowered to contribute. In my vision of becoming a company officer, I would strive to embody these traits. I would emphasize a supportive environment where team members could express their thoughts and ideas freely, fostering not just a sense of belonging but also driving collective success.

Additionally, I recognize the significance of leading by example; my actions would align with my values and the company's mission, reinforcing a strong ethical foundation. Reflecting on these traits of good officers and the experiences I had working with them has only fueled my ambition to step into a leadership role. I believe that by implementing this list of leadership qualities, I could make a meaningful impact and cultivate a positive, dynamic workplace culture. It's exciting to think about the possibility of shaping a team's future while embodying the aspects of leadership that I've come to cherish. A few colleagues and I decided, after about a year on the job, that Lieutenant was our career goal. Not that being a career driver-engineer isn't a valuable and rewarding career, but for us, LT was the gig.

I enjoyed that time coming up the ranks and took pride in using my seniority to try different styles of leadership as I got more senior. Although I made numerous mistakes, I hope to have learned from them and adapted my leadership style to improve for the next time. Getting better is what takes work. Recognizing where you need to improve and how to get there.

If you are part of a fire department or company that has a dedicated training budget, you'll likely find plenty of opportunities to enhance your skills and knowledge. The fire service is rich with state-approved curricula tailored explicitly for various roles, including operating a fire truck and obtaining officer certifications. These courses are not just options; in many departments, they can be mandatory for career advancement, serving as a critical requirement for promotions. However, even if they aren't strictly necessary, investing time in these classes can significantly bolster your resume, making you a more competitive candidate for higher positions.

Furthermore, fire service education extends beyond traditional classroom settings. Firefighters often attend seminars and conferences that can provide valuable insights, sometimes comparable to certified courses at local colleges. These events not only deliver crucial knowledge but also create networking opportunities with other professionals, encouraging collaborative learning and sharing best practices.

Beyond formal training, though, some of the most beneficial learning experiences stemmed from this peer-to-peer education. Throughout my career, I found immense value in the knowledge exchanged through conversations with colleagues who were navigating similar career paths or with fellow officers once I had moved up in rank. Engaging in discussions about real-life challenges, such as handling complex 911 calls or addressing crew conflicts, often provided me with fresh perspectives on leadership and management.

These peer-to-peer exchanges are invaluable; they build a support system where individuals can safely share their concerns and experiences. By sharing personal stories—whether they involve mistakes made on the job or successes in handling tough situations—we can foster an environment of growth and learning. Not only does this approach deepen one's understanding, but it also builds camaraderie within the department as officers learn to trust and depend on one another.

Ultimately, the combination of formal training and informal discussions enriches the knowledge base within the fire service. By engaging fully in both aspects, firefighters can develop a well-rounded skill set that prepares them for the multifaceted challenges they will face in their careers, driving them to become not only proficient firefighters but also effective leaders and mentors within their communities.

I spoke a few chapters ago about a company officer who managed Gen Z shyness by having the crew eat dinner without their phones out. I learned about this not through the rumor mill, but from talking with Jeremy firsthand, and this is only one example of the many hours we spent talking about company officer leadership and sharing officer experiences. He is a Marine, but this is only one aspect of what made him a good leader; first and foremost, he leads by example.

In fact, one time after a large-scale fire he was first due at, the crew held a debrief, and he led the talk by saying he was also taking away lessons himself. That lesson was that if he had staged his rig here instead of there, it could have opened up another option of attack that he didn't consider in the moment. His willingness to learn from and be accountable for his own decisions is what made him an officer whom people respected. I always enjoyed talking about leadership with him, and he was always one of my favorite officers to network with. He definitely can be an intense guy, but there was no doubt he cared about the job. On a personal note, I've always liked him because he's the only person I know who still uses the word "schmuck" in regular conversation.

In today's connected world, individuals are no longer confined to traditional methods of learning or networking when it comes to their vocations. With the rise of technology and digital platforms, people have access to a vast array of resources that can enhance their personal and professional development.

Podcasts have emerged as one of the most popular media for acquiring knowledge and insight. Among the countless shows available online, many focus on motivation and self-improvement, providing invaluable lessons that can resonate across various industries, especially public safety. These podcasts often feature guests with diverse backgrounds, bringing fresh perspectives on leadership, growth, and resilience.

Interestingly, some of the most impactful voices in these podcasts come from fields unrelated to public safety. This highlights the universal nature of the lessons shared; concepts such as adaptability, effective communication, and emotional intelligence are applicable to numerous professions, including public safety. How often does a former military officer speak to a group of business managers? Conversely, I often see motivational self-help speakers on the podcasts of former special forces soldiers.

Listeners can take away practical advice and sometimes inspiration from these discussions, applying these principles to navigate their own career paths. By tapping into the wealth of knowledge available through these engaging conversations, individuals can cultivate their skills, broaden their networks, and foster a mindset geared toward continuous improvement. Ultimately, the integration of technology into our learning processes—whether through podcasts, webinars, or online courses—has shifted the way people approach their careers, encouraging a more holistic and interconnected view of professional growth and personal development.

Keeping this in mind, do not limit yourself to networking with only people in your profession. A great example for me was an opportunity to go see an author at a book signing. After the signing, I had the opportunity to have an engaging conversation with this author, former mob boss, and motivational speaker, Michael Franzese. I asked Mr. Franzese about mob films and TV like *The Sopranos,* and how real the deep respect shown for the boss and their decisions truly is. Many times, in these dramas, the boss makes a decision, and the crew says "yes, sir," and would never think of disobeying because their level of respect for the head of the family borders on reverence.

More specifically, I wanted to know how much of real mob life is based on this respect for the tradition of their life, and how much of their management is based on fear. He said, "In the 40s, thought 60s, it was probably 70% respect, 30% fear. But now it's 70 to 80% fear."

I asked, "Does this work?"

He replied, "No, when you lead people by fear alone, you're always taking the chance that one day, they will fear someone more than you. This is what changed in the 90s: the mob soldiers feared the FBI more than their bosses."

This is gold.

Some of the best leadership advice I've ever heard, and the event had nothing to do with the fire service or public safety. I learned this because I wanted to network and was willing to listen.

Eyes on. Hands off.

—*General Stanley McChrystal*

10

Presence vs. Micromanaging

We talked earlier about being present. One of the worst things the boss can do is hide in their office. In the 1990s era of management training, I studied what they called Management by Walking Around.

How does the boss avoid turning this presence and supervision into micromanaging?

Very few workers I have met want to be micromanaged. Nothing is worse for morale than dealing with a situation or making a decision on a scene and having the boss change everything you did. It makes the worker feel undervalued and even undercut in front of the rest of the crew. The boss needs to be available and sometimes even watch what is happening to be effective as a manager, but a good boss will draw the line at changing the decisions made by the team.

Sometimes the boss does need to act, and by being present, you can see deficiencies and step in to correct them. A great example is a conversation I had with a Captain from a big city department with whom I was training. During a discussion of leading modern firefighters or paramedics, he told me a story of an encounter he had with an unmotivated worker just a few months before.

He mentioned that one of his crew members was on trade time, and the person covering him didn't show up at shift change. They are scrambling to see if the shift is covered, and finally, someone shows up ten minutes late. When asked, the firefighter said he was coming from his prior shift and had to drive across town. They wondered why he hadn't just called and given them a heads-up that he was on the way, and no one would have cared. He said he didn't think it was a big deal and proceeded to go sit in the recliner.

The captain, after reviewing the staffing, realized he needed this senior firefighter on trade time to drive the fire engine as the normal driver was off on vacation. The captain told the trade guy he was driving the engine and to be advised that they had a different style of engine than the normal fire truck in their fleet because this was a rescue pumper with a small aerial ladder. This was the only one of these in the fleet, and this guy had never worked with it before.

After seeing the guy nod and then continue to sit in the recliner, the captain asked him respectfully to go out to the bay and check out his rig for the day. The guy gets up, the captain heads to his office, but here is the smart move: **he leaves his door open**.

This move anticipates what might happen. He anticipated this from his experience as a company officer, having paid attention to the behavior and patterns of the people he worked with. He then put himself in a position to observe and supervise without micromanaging.

As this company officer is in the office next to the apparatus floor, he is setting up his computer staffing sheet for the day, and he can hear out in the apparatus bay:

Zippppp...Boom...Zipppp...Boom...Zippp... Boom...

He knows exactly what this is; it is the roll-up doors being opened and closed. There are seven doors, and he hears seven slams. He gets up and heads back to the kitchen, where he sees the trade guy back in the recliner.

He asks, "Did you check the truck out?"

"Yup, should be good."

"You checked out a brand-new style of rescue pumper that you have never seen before in a minute and a half?"

"Yup."

While this is going on, another firefighter was setting out some ingredients in the kitchen to prepare for the day's lunch. When he hears this, he starts putting the ingredients back, walks over to the captain, and says, "Hey, Cap, why don't we do carryout for lunch today? I have a feeling it is going to be a long morning."

"Sounds good, have the crew meet us in the bay."

The crew proceeded to take the rig through its paces with the trade guy until everyone was comfortable and he was ready to handle it for the day. The crew, without being ordered to, stayed out there with this new guy and worked with him as a team to help him get comfortable in case he has to get them water at a fire later today. They showed up for this training because they cared about the team and truly wanted to be there.

All this happened because he anticipated the trouble coming, knew to keep his door open, and paid attention. He never micromanaged; he gave the worker every opportunity to get acquainted with the vehicle and only intervened when needed. This is the type of boss people want to work for.

Helicopter Boss

Whether a boss in the workplace, a teacher in the classroom (which I have experienced firsthand as my side job), or just another mom or dad at Little League, many of us have experienced a helicopter parent. Put yourself in the child's shoes, would you want a helicopter boss at work? How would you learn your job, and how would you grow into being responsible? How would you make mistakes and gain experience from them? It is better for everyone if the boss is present, but allowing others a chance to make decisions and learn from them.

Being present means being accessible and engaged with the team, providing support and guidance when necessary. It entails understanding the tasks at hand, listening to team members' ideas and concerns, and fostering an environment where everyone feels valued.

However, a crucial aspect of effective leadership is the ability to step back and allow team members to take ownership of their work. Micromanaging can stifle creativity, reduce morale, and lead to a lack of trust within the team. Instead of hovering over every detail, a good leader delegates responsibilities and allows individuals to make decisions, which encourages accountability and professional growth.

By balancing presence with autonomy, leaders can create a healthy work environment where team members feel empowered to contribute their best. This approach not only enhances productivity but also builds a stronger, more cohesive team that collaborates effectively towards common goals. Ultimately, effective leadership lies in knowing when to guide and when to step back, ensuring that team members thrive in their roles while still feeling supported. This has the added benefit of preparing the team to make decisions when the boss is not around. As an officer, I cannot be everywhere every day. Yet when I am gone, I trust that they will be ready to handle situations on their own.

Trust Them

How can a boss have the confidence to leave tasks with the team? Easy, train them up and build that trust over time. We talked about the boss being good at the job to gain the trust of the crew, and the same goes for the team. Offer them training opportunities, lead discussions, and break down new tools or techniques. After that, you can work together to build a team you have faith in.

Building trust between a boss and their team is essential for creating a productive work environment. One of the most effective ways for a boss to feel confident leaving tasks with their team is through comprehensive training and development. It all begins with recognizing that trust is not automatically granted; it is cultivated over time through consistent effort and communication.

First and foremost, like we discussed in chapter two, a boss must establish themselves as knowledgeable and competent in their role. By demonstrating expertise and a strong work ethic, they can garner respect and trust from their team members. This creates a foundation upon which the team can feel secure in the guidance and training they receive.

Training opportunities play a pivotal role in empowering team members. A boss should actively provide access to workshops, online courses, or mentorship programs that align with the team's goals and strengths. This not only enhances individual skill sets but also boosts overall team capability. Regular training sessions can be initiated to discuss new tools or techniques, enabling everyone to stay updated and engaged with the latest industry trends.

Once the groundwork is laid through trust and training, a boss can gradually delegate tasks with confidence. This involves assigning responsibilities that match team members' skills and providing them with the autonomy to make decisions. Trusting the team to execute their roles effectively empowers them and develops their problem-solving skills. When done right, training is an investment in the team's growth and does more than anything to establish a culture of trust. This also leads to higher morale and motivation. A well-trained and confident team not only improves productivity but also fosters innovation and collaboration, which are essential for long-term success. Trusting your team starts months to years before the critical decision in the field.

Know What the Crew Does

Navy Commander and nuclear submarine Captain Scott Waddle wrote a book called *The Right Thing*, which is a book on being accountable as a leader from his experiences in a tragic Navy accident. He also talks about his time training to be a commander, in which he spent as much time learning navigation, engineering, sonar, and nuclear weapons as he did leadership and navy tactics, so when he was put in charge of a sub, he understood the jobs of every person he commanded. This training never ended, and he was required to recertify on various tasks after every deployment was complete. If there was ever a question about a task or a failure of a critical piece of equipment, the captain of the ship would, of course, rely on their staff to handle it, but in the end, the commander is the fail-safe. The buck stops with the captain.

I found the captain's knowledge about the jobs of those under their command to be very interesting, as **it was the opposite of what I experienced**.

When the boss leads by their own expertise on the job, it is one of the biggest steps in the crew trusting their leader just as much as the leader trusts the crew. This was different when I hired on. I joined the fire service after a number of years working in the private EMS field. I had gone back to school to advance my EMT licensure from basic to para-medic, as many fire departments were making this change at that time. When my department made the jump from basic life support to advanced life support, it was only a few months after I joined, and I was one of only a couple of paramedics on the job. Since a few of the workers had the advanced licensure, very few of my colleagues could do my job until the current firefighter medics got sent to paramedic class and passed their state exams.

This gap in knowledge meant that few of my peers could do my job, let alone any of the bosses. In two years, we successfully licensed all firefighters who rotate on the ambulance as paramedics, which changed the situa-tion. However, the officers were not required to upgrade their licenses. This meant that until my group was able to promote to officer, none of the department leadership would have more than a cursory knowledge of what I do. It actually wasn't their fault; we were all caught up in a generational sea change in how we did business, and it would be a few years of navigating something so new.

Some officers made an effort to understand how paramedicine operates and its impact on daily routines. This included more medical treatments on scene rather than all the patients being load-and-go, having stricter inventory on the newer EMS supplies, and the increased continuing education credits we all needed to stay licensed. As is human nature, not all bosses were as understanding, and some officers never truly learned what I do or how to manage it.

It was during these first couple of years that I knew even if I promoted to officer years down the road, that I would stay up on my medic skills, be an asset to the team during a medical run, and always be able to do the job of anyone I supervised if I had to step in. I learned later on, while rare in my fire department, that this is common in the military.

I made it my mission to stay proficient in all aspects of emergency medical care. This commitment wasn't just about personal pride or professional development; it was about the responsibility I had to my colleagues and the community we served. I wanted to ensure that if I needed to step in and help, I would be ready and capable, able to perform the same duties as anyone on my team.

As I progressed in my career, I learned that this mindset, while somewhat uncommon in my fire department, was a prevailing ethos in the military. There, the concept of versatility and preparedness among leaders is deeply ingrained. Soldiers are trained not only to lead but to be able to execute the roles of those they supervise, making them more efficient and cohesive as a unit. This perspective resonated with me and reinforced my resolve to remain engaged in all aspects of my work.

I wanted to embody the principle that no matter the rank or title, true leadership means being ready to support your team in any way necessary. This philosophy has guided me, motivating me to seek continuous improvement and knowledge, ensuring that I remain a reliable resource for my team and the community, both now and into the future.

One of my favorite stories about leadership comes not from the fire service, the military, or a *Fortune 500* business, but rather a professional kitchen. Author and Chef Anthony Bourdain, in the book that made him famous, *Kitchen Confidential*, talks in great depth about what it takes to be a boss of a kitchen. The lessons are universal: knowledge, skill, fairness, presence, and trust. He writes that, in his experience, the image of the chef hoarding their recipes for no one else to see is a complete myth. If it were true, the chef would never have an hour off any day of their life. A chef must teach and then trust the team to prepare the meals when they are not there.

Bourdain goes further; he even talks about knowing every area of the kitchen. Like the nuclear submarine captain, the buck stops with them, and anything that goes wrong must be handled quickly, even if it means the chef has to step in. He tells a story of visiting a kitchen where the chef was supposed to have the night off but had to stay to handle a staffing issue, then a purchasing issue, and when about to leave, the main commercial broiler broke. With a dining room full of people and no time to call a repair guy, the chef took off his white coat, grabbed a wrench, crawled behind the broiler, and as sous chefs passed tools to him between expletives, he worked on the broiler until he was covered in grease and dirt, and it was running. And above all, the dinner service could run without interruption. Bourdain knew nothing about his culinary skills or if he was a good cook, but he stood there watching him and said, "Now *that* is a Chef!"

> Leadership is solving problems. The day soldiers stop bringing you their problems is the day you have stopped leading them. They have either lost confidence that you can help or concluded you do not care. Either case is a failure of leadership.
>
> —*Colin Powell*

11

The Crew's Trust

U nderstanding the difference between the fire service and the military is important, especially regarding hierarchy and communication. In the fire service, we focus on teamwork and collaboration rather than strictly following military protocol. While we're trained to respect authority and recognize the ranks of our officers, our culture promotes a more egalitarian approach. We are indeed a paramilitary organization.

This means that while we recognize the leadership roles within the department, those roles are more about experience, training, and the ability to command respect rather than about rigid obedience. Firefighters are taught to communicate openly and to feel comfortable sharing their thoughts and concerns with officers, which fosters a healthy working environment.

Moreover, in high-pressure situations, such as emergencies, the ability to quickly and effectively communicate can save lives. Therefore, while rank is respected, it should not hinder the flow of communication. This philosophy helps create a more efficient and cohesive team, allowing everyone to contribute their skills regardless of their position within the hierarchy. On a medical scene or a fireground, we want our people to be able to tell a chief officer what they saw and any ideas they have.

Ultimately, the relationship between firefighters and their officers is built on mutual respect rather than a strict chain of command. It ensures that everyone feels valued and empowered, which is critical in a field where teamwork can make all the difference. That respect can grow when the crew also trusts the officer.

I was promoted to Lieutenant with just about fifteen years on the job, having spent 5 years at each position before that. When people get promoted to company officer, it's common, due to habit and human nature, to accidentally refer to a new Lieutenant by their first name, as they were usually known by their first name for fifteen years up until yesterday. When this happened to me, I would not correct the person. I simply addressed people professionally, tried to do a good job, made some mistakes, and hopefully tried to learn from them. I so badly wanted to earn that respect that I never demanded that people address me by my rank. I would not correct them or even allow myself to get annoyed by it. I let it play out and let my work speak for the type of officer I wanted to be.

Now, it is possible I took this too far and maybe could have done things differently, but I so badly wanted to earn it through merit. And then, we had a fire.

This was different, though. Normally, with a fire response, the engines and ladder trucks are all dispatched at the same time and all arrive within a couple of minutes of each other. This time, we were called to a car accident, so only my engine and an ambulance were responding. While en route, we were told by dispatch that the car actually hit a house and is on fire, and so is the building. The dispatcher tones out a full response, and this meant I would be arriving four to five minutes before any other rigs, including our battalion chief, who will be the incident commander when he gets there.

This meant that as I arrived, I would be doing a size-up on the radio, laying out a strategy, and communicating that strategy to incoming rigs and providing updates and changes before the chief showed up. This involved assigning my pipeman to attack the car fire with a defensive attack, assigning the rescue crew to stretch the supply hose from the fire truck back to the hydrant and establish a water supply, and assigning the driver to assist in deploying our hose line and sending us water to hit the car. All the while, I assigned myself a walk-around of the building to assist with evacuation because it was an occupied duplex, and also made contact with the driver of the car and performed a quick triage. I communicated all these tactics to the incoming rigs and chief, carried them out, then, when the people were evacuated, my partner and I prepared for an interior attack. I had the rescue company force the door and serve as our two-out backup crew. I advised the ladder captain to assume command upon arrival, as I would be inside the house fire, having called a transition to offensive operations.

The fire was extinguished without spreading to the other part of the duplex. The occupants were safely escorted out of their homes, the driver was taken to the ER for treatment, and all firefighters returned home safely. This was done with all incoming rigs, knowing what I had and what they needed to do when they got there. Most importantly, I devised an incident plan that worked.

And this was the last day anyone on the job ever called me by my first name.

From then on, I was Lieutenant, Cap, or Sir.

Confidence Builds Trust

From this incident, I was able to trust myself more as well. When I was a new officer, I had some bosses who wanted me to run all decisions by them and questioned the decisions I made. As I mentioned before, I grew into some confidence over time and found that one of the best ways for the crew to gain trust in you is by being decisive.

I personally did not enjoy working for managers in prior jobs or officers at the fire department who would not make decisions without checking with their boss first. It made me doubt their ideas and also their ability to lead in crunch time. I doubted their ideas because, if they were solid, they would trust them and not need to run them by the chief. At first, I thought their ideas must not be good if the boss doesn't trust them. Then, through years of working in the fire service and having conversations with people in other industries, I learned many managers had a far more troubling reason for not trusting themselves: they were afraid of getting in trouble. Far too often, I've seen bosses avoid routine decisions and escalate them up the chain of command, seeking to insulate themselves from future recriminations or protect their interview score for the next promotion. In fact, I have seen bosses with twenty-five years on say to a crew, "I have never been in the chief's office yet, and I am not going to now." As I mentioned earlier, when the chief is mad, a leader stands in front of their crew during the chewing out.

Let us take a deeper dive into that statement, though. Twenty-five years and you have never been in the chief's office, twenty-five years of driving emergency vehicles through bustling traffic, thousands of decisions made in split seconds, thousands of decisions around the station using your best judgement in the moment, and never once had to be questioned? Never once had to explain your thoughts? Never once actually made an honest mistake?

The truth is, if you have never been in trouble in twenty-five years, more than likely you have been avoiding making decisions, putting the onus on someone else instead of you. If you spend a whole career and have never made a mistake, **you have been sitting on the bench.**

This is what some managers like: being put in a box, where every decision is made for them, or they simply follow a preset algorithm: if this, then that. Some bosses don't want to, or can't deal with that pressure. The pressure of giving a command and standing by it. Then, if the decision was wrong, having the courage to stand in the boss's office and say this was your fault, not the crew's.

Being confident is the best step to the crew trusting you. Of course, it helps if your decisions are actually good, but being able to make a decision speaks volumes to the troops.

One time, for example, I had to take our fire truck to our garage after a mechanical issue and wait for another station to bring us the spare fire truck. They were busy on a call, and we had to wait, which wasn't a big deal to us, but did become an issue in a few minutes. The manager of the city's maintenance garage came out and said we would need to leave because it was time for her to close the facility for the day. We informed her that we needed to wait until the spare truck arrived so we could switch equipment to that one and get back in service.

As we were waiting, a 911 call came in for our district that we could not handle, and they sent the next closest rig. We inform her again of our need to access the spare truck and let her know we would be happy to wait there alone and switch into the new truck, leave our vehicle inside, and then lock the door on the way out. She explains that other city departments in the past have forgotten to lock the door, and they have a policy not to trust anyone other than their workers to lock up due to the value of the vehicles and tools on site. I offered her my name, ID number, and supervisor's name and office phone, and permitted her to have me disciplined if I forgot to lock the door.

"I can't, it's against the rules."

At this point, another 911 call comes in that we would have been close to, so I say, "No problem. Just have your last mechanic working here stay over to supervise us."

"I'm not authorized to give out overtime."

I, befuddled, say, "You are the department head, you run this entire facility, of course, you can. I've seen the overtime form; a department head signs it."

She says, "But the finance department gets mad and tells me not to do it."

"Who gives a crap what the finance department says? It's your department and we have a job to do."

"Well, I just can't."

I say, "No, problem. I will just take the rig outside and wait for the spare and leave it outside overnight."

She says, "You can't leave it outside, it is January, the water will freeze."

"Don't worry, I'm going to drive it up to the grass and shoot water in the tank and pump from the deck gun into the river until it's empty."

"You can't do that, it's against the rules."

"You're wrong, what I can't do is stay here another five minutes, not making a decision."

This was another example of the type of leader I did not want to be.

Decisiveness Earns Respect

I've witnessed firsthand the profound respect that troops develop for a leader who displays the courage to make tough decisions. It's not just about authority or rank; it's about the strength of character and the willingness to stand firm in challenging situations or situations that can come back on you. When a leader approaches a difficult choice with transparency, confidence, and compassion, it inspires trust and loyalty among the team.

In high-pressure environments, where the stakes are often life or death or success or failure of a company, workers look to their leaders for direction and reassurance. A leader who makes a tough call – whether it's deploying people in an emergency or addressing an internal challenge around the workplace – earns the admiration of their team. The troops not only respect the decision but also the leader's willingness to shoulder the burden of that choice.

This dynamic creates a powerful bond. The courage to confront uncomfortable truths and make sacrifices can significantly enhance a leader's credibility. When troops see that their leader is willing to take risks for the greater good, they are more likely to rally around that individual, building a cohesive unit grounded in mutual respect and shared purpose.

Ultimately, respect is earned through actions, and a leader's determination to make tough decisions is a testament to their commitment to their team and the mission at hand. The result is a motivated and resilient team that trusts in its leader, ready to face challenges together.

A common example of a non-emergent decision we sometimes make is a family emergency. In a fire department, the rigs are staffed with a minimum of people, and if we lose one person, that rig is out of service and cannot answer a 911 call. Let's say a young firefighter gets a call from home, and their new baby is sick, and their spouse is taking the little guy to the emergency room. Per the rules, I am supposed to have him wait at the station. I call the battalion chief to ask permission for the firefighter to use some hours of sick time, and then wait for a replacement to come from another station, so our rig is not out of service. Or, I could say, "Go take care of your baby." Then call the chief and explain what happened. If the chief gets mad at me, then so be it. It was my decision, not the young firefighter's. Then stand by the decision.

The same goes for decisions in the field, whether on the fireground, a factory, or a construction site; being indecisive not only holds up the mission but also represents a lost opportunity for the boss to build trust with the team. When a leader hesitates, it not only delays the work but sometimes can undermine the team's confidence and morale.

Moreover, decisive action demonstrates confidence and a willingness to take responsibility. Conversely, when leaders appear uncertain, it can lead to frustrations and increase the likelihood of mistakes, ultimately compromising safety and effectiveness.

An example of my own indecisiveness from earlier in my career is something that stuck with me as a great lesson learned. I was the senior guy on a two-person ambulance. Our rear door was getting stuck and needed to be repaired. Before leaving for our garage, my officer yelled at me to "Not milk this all morning," and he better not "Catch me using this to goof off and avoid taking runs." I, of course, would never do this, but it didn't matter; this officer didn't like me, always complained about my work, and always doubted my word.

We head to our garage, and the mechanic examines the door, estimating it might take up to forty-five minutes to fix, as he needs to remove the panel. We say go ahead. I instruct our dispatcher to prioritize our last due status for any calls, ensuring that if a call comes in, the other ambulances in our fleet will be dispatched until we are the last ones left. This is different from being out of service, which means we cannot take any calls at all until the issue is fixed, and if a call comes in, a fire engine will have to take it until another rig frees up or we call mutual aid. Sometimes, out of service is needed, and staffing issues or important repairs have to be addressed, but it was a decision I was afraid to make, seeing as how I was yelled at before leaving the station.

After the mechanic removed the panel, he noted that the door was severely corroded and required the replacement of a linkage. If we didn't replace it, there was a risk that the door might not open to allow the stretcher out in the next few calls. I told dispatch we were last due, and as luck would have it, call after call came in, and we got sent on a run, being the last ambulance available. The mechanic steps out, we take the call, come back in an hour, and try again. As we are in the garage for another try to get the door fixed, another call comes in. I look at my frustrated partner and say, "I don't know what the LT would want. What should we do?" He, perplexed as much as disappointed in me, says, "I would have called the rig out of service an hour and a half ago. I don't know what you are doing."

He was right; the right decision was to call off the air, get the rig fixed the right way, and not risk having a patient trapped in it if we couldn't get the door open. It was the best decision for any patient we had, for the fleet, and for the volume of calls for the day. If the Lieutenant was mad, so be it; I could have backed up my decision to the chain of command if he ever wrote me up. Of course, I learned after he never would have, this was a bluff and a flex all along. I was too naive to see it.

If your decision is made with the best of intentions, doing what is best for the mission, then do not be afraid to defend it. Many superior officers will likely respect decisiveness over indecision, taking it into account even if it results in a trip on the carpet.

I learned this on that day and made sure not to let it happen again, even before I was promoted to officer. I also learned to call those bluffs of some bosses who always threatened to write me up for every perceived slight or minor misjudgment, having the confidence in my thought process if ever in the chief's office.

As mentioned in earlier chapters, a strong leader recognizes that while they must make quick decisions, these choices should still invite collaboration and consideration of team input. This balance can enhance team cohesion and create an environment where everyone feels empowered to contribute.

General Stanley McChrystal writes in *Team of Teams*, "The temptation to lead as a chess master controlling each move must give way to that of a gardener, cultivating rather than directing."

Being a leader transcends the traditional notions of authority and control; it embodies the art of inspiring and guiding a team toward a shared vision. True leadership involves cultivating an environment where team members feel motivated to contribute fully to the collective goal. When a leader finds themselves resorting to constant orders and directives, it often highlights underlying issues related to trust, communication, and collaboration within the team.

A thriving team is characterized by a culture that empowers individuals to take initiative and make informed decisions. Leaders play a pivotal role in establishing this culture by fostering strong relationships, promoting open dialogue, and being receptive to both praise and constructive criticism. When team members feel engaged and valued, they naturally take ownership of their tasks, which lessens the leader's need to provide constant direction.

However, the responsibility of ownership does not rest solely on the shoulders of the team. It is equally important for leaders to take ownership of their roles and the plans they devise. This means being accountable for the training and resources provided to their team members and the clarity in the directives they issue. For a team to operate efficiently, it must have a solid foundation to rely upon. This foundation is built meticulously over time, through dedicated training, coaching, and consistent guidance. Leaders must not expect their teams to navigate challenges without adequate preparation. By equipping team members with the necessary tools and knowledge, leaders often discover they have fostered a workforce willing to go above and beyond.

An effective leader is one who creates an atmosphere where collaboration and mutual support take precedence over hierarchical commands. A team dynamic rooted in respect and shared responsibility has a two-fold benefit: it enhances morale and also contributes significantly to productivity and innovation. When individuals feel that their contributions are valued and that their insights matter, they are more inclined to invest their energy and creativity into their work.

Ultimately, the goal of leadership is to nurture an environment where individuals feel empowered, recognized, and committed to the team's mission. When this is achieved, the incessant need for orders diminishes. To put it succinctly: if a leader finds themselves in a situation where they must repeatedly give orders, it often signifies a missed opportunity to cultivate an engaged and self-sufficient team. Leadership, therefore, is not merely about directing efforts; it is about creating a legacy of empowered individuals contributing toward a collective purpose.

To put it succinctly, **if you constantly have to give orders, you have already failed as a leader.**

> The supreme quality of leadership
> is integrity.
>
> —*Dwight Eisenhower*

12

Cultivate Integrity

Rules for thee, and rules for me.

In our fire department, the battalion chief who works a 24-hour shift is the shift supervisor for that day. We have three shifts, so three battalion chiefs. To help with knowing different crews, helping their ability to partake in promotional boards, and even getting to simply know the names of the rookies, our chiefs switch shifts every January, so every few years, they have worked with most of the firefighters on the department. A few years ago, in December, ahead of the transfers, I heard from a couple of guys to "look out for" this chief, Brian is his name. That "He was a stickler for uniforms" and was like a "uniform nazi". It wasn't a major criticism because he was a great officer and commanded a lot of respect, but some people felt his demand for strict uniforms was oppressive and hard to live with. I didn't know how to take this, but as I always do, I took this warning cautiously and waited to make up my own opinion.

A few weeks pass, and this chief comes to our shift and, as is customary, sits down with each Captain on their first day to lay out roles and expectations. These are always great talks to have, but this time I wanted to know if there was anything to the uniform fears.

The chief ends the meeting by saying, "Captain, have you and your crew read the rules and regs pertaining to the daily uniform policy?"

"Yes, sir, we have and are aware of it."

Chief says, "Follow it as written."

"Sir, yes, sir."

That was the last time it was ever mentioned the rest of the year.

Nothing overbearing, nothing bossy, nothing unfair— just clear, simple direction telling me what he expected of me and the crew. The way he communicated made all the difference. I understood exactly what was required, which allowed me to focus on the tasks at hand instead of second-guessing or interpreting vague instructions.

This clarity sparked a thought in me: why did other firefighters struggle with understanding the expectations laid out by their supervisors? Perhaps their previous boss had taken a more relaxed approach, and they had grown accustomed to it. Maybe they mistakenly believed that some rules weren't critical or worth adhering to. Whatever the reason, it was evident that a disconnect existed between their past experiences and this straightforward directive provided now.

When a supervisor issues a legal order, it isn't just a suggestion; it's a responsibility. Carrying it out to the best of one's ability is not only a matter of personal pride but also crucial for the entire team's success. Resistance to following these orders distracts from our overarching mission and, more importantly, sets a poor example for the rest of the crew.

In a high-stakes environment like firefighting, where safety and efficiency are paramount, adhering to guidelines is essential. When everyone is on the same page, we stream-line our operations and enhance teamwork. Each member of the crew needs to understand that their adherence to orders contributes to the overall outcome. Ignoring or questioning direct instructions can lead to chaos, misun-derstandings, and, in the worst-case scenario, jeopardize lives. Sadly, I have seen the disruption to the operation that happens when people disregard even simple orders.

Thus, I realized that it's vital not to approach these orders with skepticism but with cooperation. Embracing the structure provided by clear leadership allows us to work cohesively, respond more effectively to emergencies, and ultimately serve our community better. We are all part of a larger mission, and our ability to follow through on expectations plays a key role in achieving our goals as firefighters. If the manager gives you a legal order, carry it out to the best of your ability. If the order was wrong or ill-advised, it can be addressed professionally during a debrief or a private meeting with the chain of command.

Arguing an order or even ignoring it is just a distraction to the mission and does not lead by example.

By facing the same challenges and following the same guidelines, a manager gains firsthand insight into how these rules affect team dynamics and individual performance. When the boss goes through the same procedures, they are better able to empathize with their team members. They can understand how certain policies might improve workflows or, on the other hand, how they can create obstacles that slow productivity. For example, if a team experiences delays because of a specific procedure, a boss who has also gone through that process can relate to their frustrations and see the need for improvement. Then the boss can advocate for them to the higher-ups with this firsthand experience.

Moreover, this shared experience bolsters communication between the boss and the team. If there's an issue with an order, for example, the boss understands the intricacies involved and can respond more effectively. They can address the team's concerns with increased sensitivity and knowledge, advocating for their needs with higher management because it is now backed by personal experience. This not only ensures that the team's voice is heard but also reinforces the boss's role as an ally.

What is most important is that when leaders model the behavior they expect from their teams, it cultivates an atmosphere of respect and accountability. A boss cannot be surprised when their crew doesn't want to wear their button-up uniform when the boss is wearing an off-duty hoodie all day. The leader, following the same rules, encourages open dialogue and promotes a culture where feedback—both positive and constructive—is welcomed. Ultimately, it empowers the entire organization to grow and adapt, fostering a culture of trust because they see that the rules are important for the boss as well.

Being Fair

"Treat everyone fairly, but you don't always have to treat them equally."
— Jimmy Johnson, NFL coach

One thing that is very unique about the fire service is your rookie year. For one, there are some legalities involved. During the first year, you are an at-will employee, so the probation is real and not ceremonial. If you are not working out, the fire chief can let you go and call it, ending the application process. After the probation is complete, a municipality now needs to show cause or go through a civil service process to terminate someone. This pressure is enough on its face, but probation comes with more challenges than just that.

Many departments use probation as a true trial period, as you rotate crews the first year, they get to judge and critique your work and you as a person. We don't expect them to be at an expert level, and sometimes, just fresh out of school, they will need even more help. The unique thing is that we don't just judge you on the work you do on 911 calls; we want to see what kind of worker you are. Are you hardworking, a team player, and can you be counted on and trusted?

To facilitate this evaluation, we have a lot of "unwritten rules" in the fire station. We encourage rookies to stay busy throughout the day with their equipment and rig check-offs, as well as practicing with tools, cleaning, or organizing supplies. It demonstrates effort and initiative, providing them with an opportunity to learn the station and showing us that they are willing to work hard. This is important because, although many of the runs we go on are routine, when we do get a fire or extrication, it is genuinely back-breaking labor. Seeing a rookie staying busy practicing with the engine, ladder, helping the cook, or just studying, shows us this is someone we can trust.

This is crucial. I have watched many interviews with members of Navy SEAL teams who say they would prefer a person who barely meets their physical standards but is highly trustworthy over someone who is extremely fit but they do not trust. It's the same for the fire service: when we give an order on a house fire, I will go about my tasks assuming that the order will be carried out. If not, the whole operation is at stake, and sometimes our safety.

For instance, if I assign a crew member to de-energize the house by pulling the electric meter, and you choose not to because it's more fun to go inside, our safety is compromised if the water streams hit exposed wires. We have to trust you will know your job, trust that you have been practicing your skills, and trust you can carry out orders. Trust is a fundamental element of our work, and it underpins every decision we make in the field.

Completing a probationary year is a crucial step in our evaluation process, one that allows us to thoroughly assess your skills, dedication, and initiative in a real-world setting. This period serves not only as a time for assessment but also as an opportunity for growth and development. It ensures that both you and the organization have ample time to adapt, learn, and confirm that this is the right fit for everyone involved.

Moreover, successfully navigating the challenges of the probationary year is an achievement in itself. It signifies your commitment to excellence and your ability to meet the expectations set before you. We want our newcomers— our rookies—to feel a sense of pride in successfully completing this journey, as it reflects not only their hard work but also their potential for future contributions to the team, and because it is a real accomplishment.

In essence, the probationary year is more than just a formality; it is a foundation upon which your career with us can thrive. It allows you to demonstrate your capabilities while also gaining valuable insights into the culture of a fire department. We celebrate this milestone and look forward to recognizing your accomplishments as you move from probation to becoming a full-fledged member of our team.

Now, once off probation, that hard work doesn't stop. We still expect people to work hard and be good team members, but we can make the job more comfortable and relaxed if you've earned it. There are some cool job perks in the fire service. If your work is done, we allow you to take a break, sit down, and unwind. We have a gym and actually encourage people to work out on duty. You can spend hours a day studying promotional books and not have to do it on your day off. These, however, are things we might not allow a rookie with one month on the job to do. The rookie is still proving themselves, but the other crew members, hopefully with years on the job, have earned those perks and breaks. It is fair sometimes to treat people differently based on their experience and contributions.

In our department, we have set promotions based on staffing, so many firefighters, senior firefighters, engineers (fire truck drivers), lieutenants, and captains. The first two ranks rotate the staffing on the ambulances and the back of the fire trucks, while the engineer solely drives the fire truck and is no longer on the ambulance. That engineer usually has about ten to twelve years on the job when that promotion happens, and has the respect that goes with that much time. When driving the fire truck, they are now up front with the officer and get to hear the officer's thoughts and feelings on whatever the topic of the day is.

So, in many ways, the engineer becomes more of an insider than the junior crew members, as much by proximity as by the trust that goes with the promotion. The engineer is also outside the fire, pumping at the rigs, and has an overall view of the fire scene. This perspective gives them great insight into how the tactics and strategy worked or could be improved. Because of this insider access and knowledge, a deeper level of trust happens between the officer and their engineer. So, to borrow a phrase from everyone's favorite film, *Goodfellas,* we call them and officers "made guys."

You always want to be fair, but not everyone is equal. Every day, we are required to hold a roll call meeting in the kitchen. The crew is allowed to grab some coffee, meet with the outgoing crew member they are relieving, or even follow up on some equipment issues, but for the most part, they know to start their day by reporting to the kitchen after the meeting is called over the PA. On one crew I was part of, we had an engineer who just got "made," and I noticed every morning he liked to start his day with a bowl of oatmeal. Most every morning, he knew to get his breakfast going before the meeting and was ready at the table with the rest of the crew. If there was ever a problem with his truck and he got pulled away, he would skip the oatmeal and wait until the end of the meeting.

But if he had to deal with a truck issue that was quick and was in the kitchen microwaving his oatmeal, and we sat down to our meeting, I was comfortable letting him wait the one minute to finish up his morning routine and join us when done. He was in the room and could hear and participate, but was allowed this courtesy because, with over fifteen years on, he has a track record of hard work and being a team player. I never minded because he is always very professional and someone we could count on. Plus, with him driving the fire engine, our getting to the scene safe and with reliable water is in his hands; it's in our interest to provide him with a comfortable work environment. For him, this meant oatmeal with green apples every morning.

I have found that being fair but flexible with assignments and duties creates a dynamic and positive work environment that significantly boosts employee motivation and engagement. When workers see that their hard work is recognized and rewarded, it fosters a strong sense of purpose and commitment to their career. This recognition can be particularly crucial for junior firefighters, who often go through long periods of rigorous training and demanding tasks before they advance in their roles.

The notion of having a "light at the end of the tunnel" not only encourages them to persist through early challenges but also instills a belief that their efforts will eventually lead to personal and professional growth. This perspective can be incredibly motivating, as it helps them envision their future success and appreciate the journey they're on.

It's essential, however, to maintain a standard of fairness in how assignments are distributed and how rules are applied. There's a risk involved in favoring certain individuals over others or creating an environment where younger members feel overburdened while others receive preferential treatment. An equitable approach ensures that all team members feel valued and supported, reinforcing the team's unity and cooperative spirit.

Moreover, offering perks and rewards for those who have proven themselves encourages a healthy competitive spirit among team members. Such incentives can take various forms, from additional training opportunities and leadership roles to special projects. This approach promotes personal accountability and inspires everyone to work their utmost, knowing that their dedication and hard work will lead to promotional opportunities with not only small pay raises but also tangible benefits. This is common in the fire service; there is only so much money a city or state can afford to pay you, and there is no equity, partnership track, or stock options to incentivize people with multiple six-figure salaries. Sometimes, the real-life incentives of benefits and job perks are just as motivational.

Ultimately, the hope is that this model of leadership will enhance individual morale and productivity, but also strengthen the overall effectiveness of the team. It results in a culture where all members strive to support one another, share knowledge, and work collaboratively towards common goals, resulting in a powerful and cohesive team for whatever job you give them.

You never want to have rules for some and different rules for others; we will always work as a team. But it does mean that people who have earned it can enjoy some perks.

"

Anyone can hold the helm

when the sea is calm.

—*Publilius Syrus*

"

13

Breach of Trust

I got asked a tricky question during a promotional interview a few years back. I had not thought about it before, but after thinking for a moment, I spoke from the heart and found out my answer resonated with that oral board and ended up being something that I used as a compass for how I would lead people going forward.

The board asked me what I would do if I caught a young crew member lying.

While I did not have an answer prepared, I did reflect on my views on leading people and said I would not get mad, at least at first. My immediate response is to wonder what I did to cause it. What did I do with my leadership style or communication that led this young man to think that he needed to fear the truth? Why was he more afraid of the consequences of the truth than the consequences of being dishonest?

As a leader, you first have to rule out those other factors before blowing your stack on this guy. Too many times, I have had a boss barking, if not shouting, orders at me at a pace that I could not completely understand or process. When questioned, I was so confused and befuddled (and young and naïve) that I stammered any response just to get the shouting to stop. When asked again, I couldn't even remember what I said before, let alone have any consistency with my statements.

Sometimes a boss can be vague in the orders they give out, leading to confusion. Other times, a poor manager can send mixed signals about what those orders are, leading to contradictions in the message. Many times, though, a heavy-handed tyrannical boss leads by intimidation rather than respect, and a young worker is so frightened of the fallout of any perceived misstep that they panic and will do anything to avoid that wrath.

The situation of an employee being caught lying on the job raises all of these important questions about accountability, the broader context within the organization, and even your leadership. First and foremost, it's necessary to evaluate the motivations behind the employee's actions. Was the lie a result of pressure to meet unrealistic expectations, inadequate resources, or a lack of support from management? Or in my case, poor communication.

If we consider the work environment, management plays a crucial role in shaping the culture and expectations. Are there issues with communication, clarity of responsibilities, or a lack of trust between employees and management? Are these things that a manager can improve on? It's essential to assess if the employee felt compelled to lie due to fear of repercussions or a belief that honesty would hinder their job performance or security.

Additionally, think about whether there are systemic problems that contribute to such behaviors. Is there a culture of fear or competition that discourages transparency? Are there proper channels for employees to voice their concerns or report issues without fear of punishment? Does the young worker not trust *you* for some reason?

Ultimately, while the individual is responsible for their actions, it is equally important to analyze how management practices and the work environment may have contributed to the situation. By addressing these underlying issues, the organization can work towards creating a more positive culture that encourages honesty and accountability.

To be honest, in a municipal fire department, it is actually hard to get fired. You really have to mess up. Part of this has to do with how hard it is to find qualified people willing to work a thirty-year career, but many times, the city knows it is a hard job with specific challenges. We routinely have to counsel a member for an EMS or a driving issue. These are difficult and unpredictable scenes, and it is common to put a scratch in the rig or have a documentation issue on the ambulance. We want our people free to make decisions in the field, and if our legal department canned people willy-nilly, it would paralyze the operation. So, we coach our new people to always be honest and not hide their mistakes. We expect mistakes and want you to learn from them.

Because of these factors, fire department leadership understands that a zero-tolerance policy for mistakes could create a stifling environment that hampers performance.

Instead of fostering fear of reprimand, the emphasis is placed on accountability and learning. New recruits receive thorough training not only in technical skills but also in cultivating a mindset that values honesty. They are encouraged to acknowledge their mistakes openly rather than hiding them, as this approach allows for growth and improvement.

Often, the crew returns from a call, reports an issue in the office, and may also anticipate a potential complaint from the patient or ER nurse. Whether it is a drug given, a dosage given, or a hospital destination chosen, as long as they had the patient's best interest in mind, then it doesn't matter what happened; I just need to know what did happen, honestly, so I can let the front office know and so no one is blindsided. If, in the end, it turns out the crew did make a mistake, then it's simple: we learn from it. Many times, the crew is not at fault as well; either way, honesty is the path away from trouble.

The culture within the department is thus built around support and guidance. Experienced members play a critical role in mentoring newcomers. They share insights on how to manage incidents successfully and help them navigate the procedural and operational hurdles that come with the job. This collaborative approach ensures that when errors do occur, they are viewed as opportunities for learning, not as grounds for punishment. Add to that, many times, the punishment is just documenting education.

Moreover, by fostering an environment where team members feel safe to communicate openly about their challenges, the department enhances its overall efficiency and effectiveness. If personnel know they can discuss their mistakes without fear, they're more likely to seek advice, ask questions, and collaborate with their peers, ultimately leading to better outcomes in the field.

The fire department, like many modern businesses, prioritizes the well-being and development of its personnel. Through coaching and a culture of honesty, they create a resilient workforce capable of making effective decisions in dynamic and sometimes chaotic situations that characterize emergency response. Ultimately, this philosophy not only maintains morale but also strengthens the team's capability to serve the community effectively.

Unfortunately, not every boss prioritized morale when I began my career. As I've mentioned before, some officers believed that I was solely interested in the paycheck and willing to tolerate anything to keep my job. This adherence to outdated management philosophies created situations and stressors that contributed to the dishonesty we've discussed.

As a result, the workplace was filled with stressors that affected not only productivity but also integrity among the team. The culture of neglect and indifference towards morale fostered an atmosphere where dishonesty not only happened but also could thrive. Employees felt undervalued and unappreciated, which led to a lack of trust and communication.

In such an environment, it becomes difficult for individuals to feel motivated to put forth their best effort, and they may resort to dishonest behavior to save their jobs and also as a coping mechanism to navigate the pressures they face. In today's fire service, we tell rookies on day one, "You're not going to get fired if anything happens on a call, just tell me about it and I will work to protect you."

" A competent leader can get efficient service from poor troops, while on the contrary an incapable leader can demoralize the best of troops.

—*John J. Pershing*

14

Walk with Purpose

Empathy, compassion, caring, listening, and presence. Where do you start?

There is no right way or one single way to lead. For me, however, I have always started by getting to know your team. Learn about them and their strengths and weaknesses, if any. Find out what they do well, and find out if they even need you to make any changes. Often, they're a great crew and doing well before you arrive, so the "new sheriff is in town" isn't necessary. Even if it is, take some time to learn and observe before making whole-sale changes.

In most cases, you do not need to come in and walk tall and demand respect. It's almost the opposite; give the crew the respect they deserve for doing the work before you arrived. If you're brought in to address issues and problems, take the time to get to know the team before making significant changes. You will be surprised to learn that even if there are problems you were brought in to fix, the people are genuinely good workers at heart who just need some fine-tuning. Providing them with that respect from the beginning is a great way for you to earn respect.

In most of these cases, it's essential to approach a new situation with humility rather than an air of superiority. When stepping into a new role or environment, especially one where you have been called in to address problems, it's crucial to remember that the team in place has likely been doing their best under challenging circumstances. Instead of walking in with the mindset of demanding respect or immediate changes, consider the power of giving the existing crew the respect they deserve for their ongoing efforts and contributions. Many times, if they are off track a little, it's because of their hard work that things haven't gone completely off the rails. Give them the credit for that.

Start by fostering open communication with your team. Take the time to get to know them—not just their work habits, but also their individual strengths, challenges, and perspectives. Establishing a rapport with your colleagues can provide you with invaluable insights into the situation at hand. You may find that the problems you were brought in to solve are layered and complex, rooted in broader issues rather than simple incompetence.

In many instances, the people you're working with are genuinely dedicated and skilled workers who simply need guidance, support, and perhaps a fresh perspective. Instead of implementing drastic changes right away, assess the environment and recognize the potential that already exists within the team. By validating their experiences and acknowledging their hard work, you create a foundation of trust and collaboration.

Providing this respect from the very beginning helps you earn their trust in return. When team members feel valued and understood, they are more likely to be open to constructive feedback and more willing to embrace change. This mutual respect fosters a positive atmosphere where creativity and problem-solving can thrive, ultimately leading to better outcomes for the organization.

When asked to manage people in challenging situations, it is not just about correcting course but about building relationships. Show your team that you are there to support and uplift them, and you will find that respect is reciprocated, fostering a more productive and steady work environment.

Even with the support you show the team and the respect you give them, there will still be times when you need to take charge. While people don't want a micromanager, they certainly won't want to be led by someone afraid to assume responsibility. Be willing and able to make decisions, and yes, sometimes aspire to being the decision maker. You wanted to be a boss for a reason, and when situations warrant it, you need to be comfortable taking command.

Leadership is not just about guiding others; it's also about being decisive and willing to make tough calls when the situation demands it. Effective leaders must be prepared to embrace their role as decision-makers, understanding that this is often a key part of their responsibilities.

The reason you aspired to a leadership position in the first place is likely linked to your desire to influence outcomes of the job you do, inspire people, and navigate challenges. When the moment arises to lead decisively, seize the opportunity with confidence. This means being informed, weighing options carefully, and ultimately choosing a path that aligns with your team's training and preparation, goals, and the organization's mission.

In the previous chapter, we discussed developing people into a team; now, you can focus on cultivating your leadership style. Hopefully, this style strikes a balance between support and assertiveness, because it helps you earn your team's trust and empowers them. They will respect your ability to handle complex situations and appreciate that you can make tough decisions when needed. In doing so, you promote a culture of accountability and collaboration, which are vital for high-performing teams. Remember, leadership is just as much about guiding your team through collective successes as it is about leading them through difficult times.

It is kind of a management buzzword, but I really believe command presence is a tangible thing. Being assertive does not have to be about shouting orders on the battlefield. Good leaders can command respect by the way they carry themselves. Are you professional in how you act, or always joking with the crew? While humor can lighten the mood, it's essential to strike a balance between being approachable and being taken seriously. A good leader knows when to be casual and when to adopt a more serious tone, adapting their approach based on the context and the needs of the team.

Do you have a grasp of the job, or are you always asking the junior members how things work? If you find yourself frequently seeking guidance from junior members, it can create uncertainty within the team. While it's perfectly acceptable to ask questions and maintain a learning mindset, having a solid grasp of the tasks at hand establishes your credibility. It demonstrates that you have the experience and knowledge necessary to guide your team effectively.

Do you speak clearly with focus and intent, or do you ramble and obscure your message? Clear, focused, and intentional speech conveys confidence and aids in preventing misunderstandings. If you tend to deliver messages in a vague manner, it can lead to confusion and a lack of direction. Being articulate and concise not only helps ensure that your message is understood but also reinforces your position as a capable leader.

At its core, command presence refers to the ability of a leader to project confidence, authority, and decisiveness. This isn't just about being the loudest voice in the room or barking orders; it encompasses a range of qualities that inspire respect and trust among team members.

Ultimately, command presence is not about standing tall and being loud. It is about embodying the qualities that inspire others to follow. It combines professionalism, knowledge, effective communication, and the ability to engage with your team in a meaningful way. By consciously developing these attributes, leaders can foster a more motivated and cohesive team, ready to tackle challenges head-on.

I have a friend who used to work with the Detroit Tigers major league baseball team. During the 2000s, they were one of the best teams in the majors and made two World Series. The owner, Mike Ilitch, was one of the most respected businessmen in metro Detroit ever. Successful, famous, and well-liked. At this time, he was slowing down and turned the day-to-day over to the family, but still had a presence in the building. The general manager, Dave Dombrowski, was one of the most well-respected GMs in the league, having won a World Series and taken three teams to the finals. (now it is 5).

This person was telling me about the year-end party the office staff was having at their offices at the ballpark when she mentioned she heard Mr. Ilitch had come by and was sitting with his family. She then said she was excited to learn Mr. I was there and couldn't wait to find him to say hello. I asked if Dave Dombrowski attends office parties like this, and she said yes, he was there.

"Would you ever ask if Mr. Dombrowski was there and see if you could find him to say hi?"

She said, "Oh, that would never happen."

"In what way?"

"Everyone knows when Dave Dombrowski walks into a room."

Whether it's how you move, how you stand, your tone of voice, your choice of words, or command presence, it's real and the troops will notice it.

One time, we had a house and garage fire, and we were second due. As I approach the scene, I see the first due crew setting up hoses, the engineer charging lines, and preparing to hook to a hydrant, while the rescue crew moves to the front door. It was 3 a.m., and dark with the glare of the emergency lights making it hard to see through the haze of the drifting smoke. As I walked past the driveway, nearing the back of the ladder truck with my partner, the chief radios for me to grab a piece of equipment off the back of the ladder truck and go to the side of the building and deploy it. After completing this task and assisting with the fire operations for the next hour, I went to the chief and said, "That worked out. I was right there when you gave me that task."

"It wasn't luck, I saw you there, so I gave you that order."

"How did you know it was me? It's dark and hazy, I can only see vague shapes."

"I knew it was you. You walk with a purpose."

So, I got that going for me, which is nice.

His words, though, stuck with me, and I felt a sense of pride when I heard them as much as if I had received an "AttaBoy" letter in my personnel file. While I'm far from perfect, it's reassuring to know that I carry myself in a way that others recognize. It was a small acknowledgment of my dedication and determination in such high-pressure moments. In our line of work, every detail counts, and I strive to walk with that same purpose, not just for myself but for my team and the community we serve. It's that unwavering commitment that drives me to keep improving, to keep learning, and to be ready for whatever challenges lie ahead.

Be Your Own Leader

Being a good boss goes beyond reading books, listening to lectures, and taking management classes; it has to come naturally. You have to believe in it and truly want to do it. It needs to be an inherent part of your personality where the empathy and care you have for the troops are something deeply personal to you.

The essence of effective leadership tends to stem from a deeper, more intrinsic motivation. It's about embodying the principles of leadership in your day-to-day interactions and operations. A true leader must genuinely believe in the importance of their role.

This belief transforms into an authentic desire to support and uplift their team. When leadership is approached from a place of intrinsic passion, it fosters an environment of trust and respect. This commitment should feel like a natural extension of one's personality, rather than just a set of professional responsibilities.

We have discussed empathy many times in this book, yet genuine empathy is at the core of effective management. It involves not just understanding your team's needs but also genuinely caring about their well-being, both professionally and personally. Not caring because it says so in some book, but because caring is actually at your core. Good bosses recognize that their team members are individuals with their own aspirations, challenges, and emotions. When a leader connects on this personal level, it creates a strong bond that enhances collaboration and loyalty.

As I've said before, a good leader actively seeks to promote an inclusive atmosphere where every team member feels valued and heard. This connection fosters open communication and encourages team members to voice their ideas and concerns without fear of judgment. Such a culture not only boosts morale but can also lead to enhanced creativity and problem-solving within the team. Being inclusive also means sharing the credit if your teams have great ideas. If you are the boss, you probably have enough credit over your career; it's time to share the wealth.

Ultimately, the best leaders are those who understand that their leadership is not merely a role to fulfill but a profound responsibility to their team. They aim to inspire, mentor, and guide rather than to command or control. In doing so, they cultivate a team that feels empowered and motivated to achieve shared goals, resulting in a more engaged and productive workplace. More importantly, a leader must want this responsibility and have it be part of their deeply held beliefs. The crew will see through a boss who is pretending to care because they read it in a book.

One of the most interesting examples of failing at these basic principles of leadership is the Costa Concordia cruise ship accident. For those not familiar, the Costa Concordia was a major cruise liner that ran aground and fell sideways along the Italian coast while the captain was attempting a showy "fly by" maneuver for the beach goers, and possibly some female guests on the bridge.

After the ship ran aground and tilted sideways, it submerged halfway in the water, and people were thrown about; an evacuation was called for all the passengers. Thirty-two people died in the accident, and countless others had to be rescued due to injuries that prevented them from evacuating on their own. As the ship was sideways, the lifeboats could not all be deployed due to the angle, so rescue boats raced to the scene to begin evacuations.

During the hectic first hour of evacuations, the captain of the ship boarded a rescue boat and left.

Four thousand people still needed to get off the boat, and the captain left on one of the first Coast Guard vessels to arrive. As the emergency unfolded, the remaining officers and crew remained at their posts, the port authority and coast guard sprang into action and coordinated rescue and evacuations, and the passengers all waited as calmly as possible to board lifeboats. All of this took place without the captain.

In reading about and seeing the incident unfold on television, the most fascinating part was in a port authority center on shore, where the captain was recognized and brought to a radio. The conversation that happened between the captain and the Coast Guard dispatcher was eye-opening and even shocking. It was all in Italian, but reading the translation, the dispatcher asked the captain why he wasn't on board. The captain stammered an excuse about needing to supervise the lifeboat evacuations.

The dispatcher told the captain in no uncertain terms that he must get back on the ship and resume command. The captain said he could command the evacuations from the shore and staging area.

The dispatcher then, in a wonderful and calm voice, told the captain he understood there might have been some initial confusion and chaos, and that, in haste, a mistake was made. Yet, now with time to reconsider, he needs to be back with his crew. The coast guard has another boat leaving for the ship in a moment, and he can provide him a ride to the scene. He can then resume command, and this will be forgotten.

The captain still refused and insisted on his failed and meek attempt to assume any command from the safety of shore.

What is fascinating about this story is that pulling the reckless shoreline 180-degree maneuver that grounded the ship wasn't the worst thing that happened. Even with that, if he had taken responsibility and properly supervised the entire rescue, he could still have salvaged a career sailing a ship full of rubber dog crap out of Hong Kong.

But he didn't.

He abandoned the ship and four thousand passengers.

This was the thing that was unforgivable. It not only led to his ostracization from the maritime community, but it also led to criminal prosecution. But more than just the laws of maritime conduct, this was a betrayal of everything that is supposed to be innate in a ship's captain. The true, inner to your core belief that it is the absolute duty of anyone who accepts the role of captain of a ship, will always be the last off the ship, up to and including going down with it.

So deeply ingrained in the culture of marine and naval officers is the notion that the captain never abandons their passengers; the criticism and shock of horror over this action were immediate and universal across the globe.

Once again, the leader has to want to be there, has to believe in the mission, and has to care more about the crew than themselves. It is essential that this becomes an integral part of who you are as a person, making it truly second nature.

" A leader is best when people barely know
he exists, when his work is done,
his aim fulfilled, they will say:
we did it ourselves.

—*Lao Tzu*
"

Conclusion

One great thing about the Internet age is the ability to learn. Learn new things, learn from new people, learn from different types of people. Whether it be online magazines or podcasts, leadership is now a topic that has many platforms and even more people sharing their lessons. Gone are the days when management of people was only learned from college coursework or the ghost-written memoirs of Fortune 500 CEOs. People who aspire to lead can learn from former military special forces soldiers, self-help authors, entrepreneurs, and yes, even a simple fire captain.

I hope you enjoyed this book, but don't ever stop searching for more opportunities to broaden your knowledge. Whether it's books like this or podcasts and social media, there is a vast array of voices contributing to the discussion. The web has democratized a topic like leadership. If you are willing to go look for it, aspiring leaders now have access to wisdom and strategies from a wide range of experts.

In a fun coincidence, and a great example of being available to listen and learn at all times, as I was taking a break from writing this last chapter, I went for a run and listened to an interview with actor Jeff Goldblum. When asked what it takes to be a professional actor with a long career, he said, "It takes a decade or two of hard work. Then a lifetime of continuing that work."

Leadership should not be any different.

To come full circle, I started this book talking about the bad bosses I had. Many times, it was not their fault. It was just what they knew. I don't hold a grudge. In fact, I feel grateful that I was provided with both good and bad opportunities to learn. I worked with some great firefighters and medics coming up the ranks, and we all had experiences to share and collectively learn from. That peer-to-peer learning allowed all of us to point out these examples, and as a group of young firefighters, we made the conscious decision to be better.

There is no reason to treat the people under you a certain way just because that's what you had to deal with.

I'll end with one of my favorite quotes: Marcus Aurelius said, "The best revenge is to be unlike your enemies."

Acknowledgments

It's a strange feeling to wrap up this project. It was challenging, hard, and enjoyable, and I will miss it. Writing a book was something I always said I would "do one day." After many false starts, stops, and dead-end ideas, I finally found a topic I knew well and was passionate about. While I had numerous thoughts and lessons that flowed out of me, it was a challenge to organize them into coherent chapters. Despite the effort I put into it, I miss the evenings spent at the computer, sharing my thoughts on the page. I also miss the sip of bourbon I would treat myself to as a reward for a productive night.

As I mentioned in the foreword, I could not have completed this work without the skilled guidance of my editor, Michael Tizzano. While authors may be experts in their field and express their thoughts from the heart, grammar, style, and structure are entirely different disciplines. I also found reading your own writing with a critical eye is nearly impossible. It all sounds perfect as you read it to yourself. I guess the brain sees what it wants to see. It is always a shock to get an edited work back and see how many red lines are scattered through every single paragraph, no matter how many times I proofread it. Thanks again Michael.

I also want to take a moment to express my heartfelt gratitude to my children, Isabella and Zachary, for being such wonderful kids. Being a firefighter and paramedic is truly the best job in the world, but I have to say that being a dad surpasses even that joy. I am so proud of the way they have embraced my profession; they have always shown excitement and pride about having a firefighter as their dad. Whenever I had to leave for my 24-hour shifts, their support meant the world to me.

One of the great benefits of working in the fire service is that even though my shifts are long, they provide me with more days off each month than many other jobs. This flexibility has allowed me to be more involved in their lives. I've relished the opportunity to volunteer for school trips, attend band competitions, and coach Little League teams. This, on top of being able to pick them up from school many days, and cook dinner for our family. Each of these experiences has created lasting memories for me.

I will always remember the many occasions when their mom would bring them to the fire station. Seeing their faces light up as we took pictures together, with them in my firefighting gear, wearing the helmet, or beside the fire truck, are moments I will always treasure. Those experiences not only brought us incredible memories but also instilled in us a sense of pride and admiration for the work that I do. I am grateful for those moments with them.

When I began my career in the fire service, there were two major monthly trade magazines that many firefighters relied on to share new ideas, learn techniques, and express opinions. However, this landscape has changed significantly over my career.

One of my favorite developments in our field is the emergence of an entire online and social media community dedicated to education and discussion related to fire and EMS. In the past, we would occasionally receive grainy VHS footage of incidents, which would be included in training videos that repeated the same material because of the lack of film of real fire incidents.

Now, every fire occurring across the country is often filmed on cell phones and posted on social media, creating a vibrant community where discussions about fire tactics and strategies happen daily. Additionally, firefighters are sharing helmet cam footage, providing us with an endless supply of not only exterior fire behavior but also interior conditions. This offers invaluable learning opportunities for firefighters nationwide.

The exploration of these social media pages, podcasts, and YouTube channels has profoundly enriched our understanding of various tactical issues that affect our fields. They provide insights from diverse perspectives, allowing us to analyze challenges and develop innovative solutions.

Moreover, these platforms have become breeding grounds for discussions surrounding leadership. Engaging with the content and participating in the conversations has inspired me to reflect deeply on my own views regarding leadership. I've come to realize that effective leadership is not just about making decisions, but also about inspiring others, fostering collaboration, and creating an environment where everyone feels valued.

By sharing my thoughts and experiences related to leadership, I hope to contribute meaningfully to these ongoing dialogues. I believe that by exchanging ideas and learning from one another, we can cultivate a stronger community of leaders who are capable of navigating the complexities of our world. It's exciting to be part of a larger movement that encourages continuous growth and development in leadership practices, and I'm eager to see where these discussions will lead us in the future.

I hope this book can be a part of those discussions.

www.ingramcontent.com/pod-product-compliance
Lightning Source LLC
Chambersburg PA
CBHW021928190326
41519CB00009B/942